W0114310

THREE CHEERS

THREE CHEERS

COCKTAILS THREE WAYS: CLASSICS, RIFFS, AND ZERO-PROOF SIPS

KAITLYN STEWART

FOUNDER OF @LIKE•A•BLE COCKTAILS

TEN SPEED PRESS

California | New York

CONTENTS

INTRODUCTION

This book is dedicated to the love of cocktails in all their many forms. Here you will find a drink to suit your every mood and occasion. Explore the world of the classics, try your hand at something new, or experience your favorite drink completely spirit-free. Whether you are a beginner or consider yourself an expert, this book will surely have something for you!

But first, allow me to introduce myself. My name is Kaitlyn Stewart, and my platform is known as Like•a•ble Cocktails. I am an award-winning bartender who was once named the best in the world! True story. I have been mixing and shaking up drinks for more than twenty years and have dedicated my life to the pursuit of the perfect cocktail.

I grew up in a hospitality family. My mom and dad met while working at a restaurant and practically raised my sister and me in booth 17. At a young age, I learned from them the importance of affability, and that it was more than just making sure people were enjoying the food and drinks they ordered—it meant going above and beyond, to exceed people's expectations and anticipate their needs. Though my love and passion for hospitality, food, and flavors was kindled as a kid in restaurants, it really started with my grandma. I have so many fond memories of sitting at the kitchen table, watching my grandma work her magic with whatever she had in the fridge. They weren't always the fanciest meals, but they certainly were always made with love. She could turn a basic TV dinner into a gourmet meal, and you'd never know the difference. My grandma was the type of person to always have an extra plate of food in the fridge just in case there was an extra person joining us at the table. She always made sure you felt welcomed.

I didn't set out to be a bartender. Like many people, I started bartending to help pay for university. I was going to school for film and television studies while bartending and teaching dance simultaneously. I worked at every type of bar and restaurant imaginable—from chain restaurants to fancy high-end hotels to nitty-gritty dive bars—which all taught me something different about bartending. It wasn't until I met my first real bar mentor, Justin Taylor, in 2014, that I learned I could turn my love for bartending into a career that would one day take me around the world. He taught me how to use cocktail making as a creative outlet and how to tell stories through flavors. He also entered me in my first bartending competition, which ended up changing my life forever.

The year was 2017, and after competing in several local cocktail competitions I decided to throw my hat in the ring for the biggest and most prestigious international bartending competition, World Class, conducted by Diageo Spirits. I had no real expectations going into this competition, but as a Capricorn I was going to do my damnedest to win! First I had to compete and win in my home country before going up against all the other countries' winners from around the world. The global finals were held in Mexico City that year, with sixty of the world's best bartenders all representing their countries and hoping to win the title of World's Best Bartender. As the weeklong competition progressed, the competitors were cut down from sixty to ten, then ten to four. It was a surreal experience even making it to the top four. And then when they called my name as the winner, I could hardly believe it. Not only was I the first Canadian to win the title of World's Best Bartender, but I was only the second female to take home the prestigious award. That moment changed the trajectory of my life forever. I started traveling all over, giving seminars to bartenders and doing guest bartending shifts at some of the world's best bars while experiencing different cultures, flavors, and forms of hospitality.

And then the pandemic hit. Which forced me, for the first time in a long time, to stay grounded and reassess what my future looked like. Was it time to get that "real job"? Hell no! I decided to turn what I was truly passionate about into my "real job." And so, Like·a·ble Cocktails was born, which helped me connect with my "regulars" and have a creative outlet. I couldn't get behind a real bar, so I brought the bar to my apartment and started making videos and uploading them to social media. I quickly realized that I could reach even more people virtually than I ever could in person. I was able to share my passion and knowledge with whoever wanted to listen. In a way, social media became a new form of hospitality for me.

My goal as a bartender has always been to make cocktails feel inclusive and accessible to everyone—and I mean everyone. From the basic vodka soda drinker to the classic cocktail lover, to the nondrinker. I want to show everyone how easy it can be to mix up a tasty drink no matter your mood. And that's exactly what I intend to do here with this book. Now, how often can you say you learned how to make drinks from one of the best bartenders in the world?

HOW TO USE THIS BOOK

So, what will you find in the pages of *Three Cheers*? I have divided the book into three easy to follow sections.

TOOLS, TIPS, AND TRICKS OF THE TRADE

Here you will find a comprehensive list of the essential tools every home bar should have, with some accessible swap-outs for when the usual equipment isn't an option. I will also go down the rabbit hole of some fun, slightly obscure bar tools that you might want to add to your next wish list. You will also find some useful tips and tricks on how to properly use your bar tools, when it's appropriate to shake vs. stir a cocktail, and some useful tips for entertaining.

This section will also include a comprehensive measurement guide to help you out with those pesky conversions. From ounces to milliliters and grams to cups, *measurements matter*!

DIY HOMEMADE INGREDIENTS AND STOCKING YOUR BAR

Here you will find all the recipes for the homemade cocktail ingredients needed for some of the cocktails in the book. From basic simple syrup to slightly more complex cedar-smoked rye, this section will be your step-by-step guide. Don't be intimidated, I'll be with you every step of the way. You will also find a breakdown on how to properly stock your home bar. From what basic spirits you should have, to bitters and glassware.

LIKE•A•BLE COCKTAILS FOR EVERYONE AT EVERY PROOF

Here you will find 165 cocktail recipes. These recipes are broken up into what I call the "holy trinity." Each page will start with a classic cocktail, followed by my variation of the classic cocktail, and finally a completely spirit-free version of the classic cocktail. From the Air Mail all the way to the Zombie, there most certainly will be a drink for everyone.

SO, WHAT ARE WE DRINKING?

TOOLS, TIPS, AND TRICKS OF THE TRADE

Bar tools are a bartender's best friend. Each tool has a specific use and purpose. It is important to know how to use your bar tools to get the most out of them. But bar tools don't make the bartender. A good bartender should be able to use whatever they have on hand at any given time. You can have the fanciest of equipment and still make a subpar drink.

5 ABSOLUTE MUST-HAVES

MEASURING JIGGER

The key to any good cocktail is consistency. And the only way you can guarantee consistency is by measuring your cocktail ingredients. There are several types of measuring jiggers: **Japanese jigger, bell jigger, multilevel jigger, OXO measuring cup jigger.**

The Japanese and bell jiggers have a dual-measure design, one side measuring 1 ounce and the other side measuring 2 ounces. Whereas the multilevel and OXO measuring cup are both a single vessel. Go with what feels comfortable to you, but keep an eye out for the capacity of each jigger. Not all jiggers are a standard 2 ounces.

Accessible Swap-out

If you don't have access to a measuring jigger, you can use baker's measuring spoons.

1 tablespoon = ½ ounce or 15 milliliters

2 tablespoons = 1 ounce or 30 milliliters

4 tablespoons = 2 ounces or 60 milliliters

COCKTAIL SHAKER

A cocktail shaker can be used for several things. First and foremost, a cocktail shaker is used to shake drinks. There are two main styles of cocktail shakers: **two-piece Boston shaker** and **cobbler shaker.**

The Boston shaker consists of two pieces, a top and bottom. I personally prefer to use a stainless steel "tin on tin" Boston shaker versus a "glass on tin" Boston shaker. With tin on tin, there is a lower chance of breakage, it is lighter weight, and it keeps your drinks extra cold.

The cobbler shaker consists of three pieces: a bottom, a top with a built-in strainer, and a cap. The cobbler shaker tends to be a bit smaller in overall capacity and sometimes a tad tricky to open.

With both the Boston and cobbler shaker, you can use the bottom piece as a mixing vessel.

Accessible Swap-out

If you don't have access to a cocktail shaker, you can use several common kitchen items in its place: a mason jar, a jam jar, or a protein shaker. Basically, anything with a sealable lid will work.

COCKTAIL STRAINER

There are two types of cocktail strainers: **julep strainer** and **Hawthorne strainer.**

The julep strainer has a very storied history. It was originally used as a type of sieve before straws were invented. The julep strainer would be positioned on top of the drink to hold back the ice while sipping. Now it is typically used to strain spirit-forward drinks, such as a martini or Negroni.

The Hawthorne strainer was patented by William Wright at the Hawthorne Café in Boston as a new and improved julep strainer. It is lined with a coiled spring to fit any glass size and to catch all the unwanted bits from going into your glass, like herbs, fruit, and ice. If I had to pick just one cocktail strainer to use, I'd go with the Hawthorne strainer.

Accessible Swap-out

If you are in a pinch, a slotted spoon or tea strainer will do the trick.

BAR SPOON

Like the measuring jigger, there are several different types of bar spoons: **American bar spoon, European bar spoon, Japanese bar spoon.**

Each of these bar spoons essentially does the same thing, stirs drinks. The American bar spoon has a twisted handle and flat spoon end. The European bar spoon has a twisted handle with a deeper spoon on one end and a flat coin on the other end for layering drinks and muddling. The Japanese bar spoon also has a twisted handle with a deeper spoon on one end and a weighted teardrop on the other for balance. Any of these bar spoons will do the trick! I personally prefer the weighted Japanese bar spoon for its comfort and glide while stirring.

Accessible Swap-out

If you don't have a bar spoon on hand, feel free to use a chopstick, the handle of a wooden spoon, or a soup spoon.

CITRUS JUICER

Fresh is always best! Store-bought citrus juice tends to be filled with shelf stabilizers and alternative acids. If you want the best results for your drinks, use a citrus juicer to squeeze fresh juice.

There are several kinds of citrus juicers: **hinged squeezers, manual countertop juicers, hand reamers, electric juicers.**

This really comes down to personal preference. I tend to use a hinged squeezer, or "elbow juicer." You get excellent results, they're easy to clean and easy to store.

Accessible Swap-out

If you don't have a citrus juicer handy, then I suggest using pure brute strength and squeezing your juice by hand. Cut your citrus into quarters and use a fork to help get as much juice out as possible.

BONUS TOOLS

If you want to take your cocktail skills to the next level, think about adding these tools to your collection as well!

ATOMIZER

A small perfume-like bottle used to reduce liquid into a fine spray. Perfect for accent spirits like absinthe or a peated Scotch whisky. It can also be used to rinse the glass or spritz over a finished cocktail.

BLENDER

A standard kitchen blender can be useful in many ways: to make frozen/slushy drinks, but also to make a quick and easy simple syrup or to crush ice for a julep-style drink.

FINE-MESH SIEVE

Typically used in conjunction with the Hawthorne strainer, the fine-mesh sieve is used to catch all the unwanted bits the Hawthorne strainer may have missed—ice chips, pulp, or herbs to name a few.

ICE MOLDS

Silicone ice mold trays are a great addition to elevate your cocktail game: 2-inch cubes are an ideal size for spirit-forward drinks, such as an old-fashioned or Negroni. The larger the ice cube, the slower the ice melts.

ISI WHIPPER

A small canister that holds liquid that can be charged with either CO_2 to create foams or NO_2 for rapid infusions.

KITCHEN SCALE

A digital kitchen scale is extremely useful when you need/want to be very specific with your measurements. Whether you are making a simple syrup by weight or adding acid to adjust a citrus juice, the precision of a scale is key.

LEWIS BAG

A basic canvas bag used to hold ice cubes for crushing.

MICROPLANE

Unlike a traditional box grater, a Microplane has much finer blades, which produces a much more consistent result. It is typically used to zest citrus fruit or grate spices, like nutmeg or cinnamon, on top of a drink.

MILK FROTHER

The milk frother is my secret weapon when it comes to cocktails made with egg whites. Instead of doing a "dry shake" (without ice), I like to use a milk frother to aerate the cocktail. This results in a very light and fluffy consistency.

MUDDLER

A long and slender tool, either wood or metal, used to crush ingredients, such as fruits, herbs, and spices in the bottom of a glass or cocktail shaker.

POUR SPOUTS

Small bottle toppers that control the flow of the liquid.

SERRATED KNIFE

Excellent for cutting through citrus fruits, the serration grips the surface, allowing for clean cuts.

VEGETABLE PEELER OR Y-PEELER

This kitchen tool is commonly used for creating strips of citrus peels for garnishes.

SHAKEN, STIRRED, BUILT, OR BATCHED

You have the tools and the recipes, so what comes next? The mixing method! But how do you decide if a drink should be shaken, stirred, or built in the glass? And does it really matter?

There are a couple of standard rules of thumb when it comes to preparing a cocktail. If the recipe is straight spirits, like a Manhattan or martini, the cocktail should be stirred. If the recipe calls for juices, purees, or dairy products, like a daiquiri or whiskey sour, nine times out of ten you're going to want to shake that cocktail. But if the drink consists of two-thirds of a mixer like soda or tonic water, it is typically built in the glass.

SHAKEN

By shaking a cocktail, you are breaking up the ice in the cocktail shaker, which in turn not only chills but dilutes your mix. Shaking also creates tiny bubbles, which gives the cocktail a frothy mouthfeel. Shaking also sufficiently agitates the mix and binds the ingredients together.

When shaking a cocktail, you want the ice to do the work for you, so don't be shy—fill your cocktail shaker up with plenty of it. Make sure your cocktail shaker is sealed tight, and with one hand on the top and one hand on the bottom, move your cocktail shaker with a fluid up-and-down motion, allowing the ice to move from the bottom to the top of the shaker with every hit. A standard cocktail should be shaken for 10 seconds or until the outside of the cocktail shaker is nice and frosty. If done correctly, the volume of your cocktail inside the shaker should increase by 20 percent.

STIRRED

Stirring a cocktail is a more delicate approach to adding chill and dilution to your mix, giving the cocktail a velvety smooth mouthfeel. Because most stirred drinks are spirit-forward, there isn't the need to agitate the ingredients, just gently "bloom" them. You can use a mixing glass or the bottom piece of your cocktail shaker as a stirring vessel. I suggest adding your spirits to the mixing glass first and your ice last. That way you have more control over the dilution rate of your cocktail. When stirring, place a mixing spoon into the mixing glass with the back of the spoon up against the outer wall of the glass. Using a circular motion with your wrist, gently rotate the spoon clockwise. For a standard cocktail, you should be stirring for 30 to 45 seconds. If done correctly, the volume of your cocktail should increase by 20 percent.

BUILT

Most built drinks are two-thirds mixer and consist of two ingredients and a garnish. For example, a whiskey highball or gin and tonic doesn't need to be shaken or stirred in order to incorporate the ingredients. The drink simply needs to be built in the glass over ice. After building your drink in the glass, be sure to give it a gentle stir just to incorporate the mix and spirit all the way through.

BATCHED

If you want to turn your favorite cocktail into a large batch, simply multiply all your ingredients equally. If you don't plan on stirring or shaking your prebatched cocktail, you can add the dilution manually (typically in the form of water) by multiplying the total volume of your cocktail by 20 percent. That will give you the proper dilution ratio you will need to add to ensure you are serving a balanced drink.

Having prebatched cocktails ready to go will make entertaining your guests that much easier. You can make batches a day or two ahead of time and store them in the fridge. When you can, leave the alcohol out of the mix and allow your guests to "choose their own adventure." Not only does it make things more inclusive for those who are not imbibing, but it allows your guests to tailor their drinks to their preferred tastes. Also, having a selection of mixers out alongside a garnish board makes for a playful "build your own" highball station.

MEASUREMENTS MATTER

Cocktails are a lot like baking. It is important to measure every ingredient to ensure a consistent and balanced outcome. If even one measurement is slightly off, it can ruin the entire drink. If you are ever unsure of a measurement, remember that less is more. You can always add, but never take away. Everyone's palate is very different. Some prefer sweet over sour or bitter over salty. By using a structured drink recipe as your base, you can then start to tailor your drinks to your specific likeness.

MEASUREMENTS CHEAT SHEET

Liquids

¼ fluid ounce	=	8 milliliters	=	½ tablespoon
½ fluid ounce	=	15 milliliters	=	1 tablespoon
¾ fluid ounce	=	22 milliliters	=	1½ tablespoons
1 fluid ounce	=	30 milliliters	=	2 tablespoons
1¼ fluid ounces	=	38 milliliters	=	2½ tablespoons
1½ fluid ounces	=	45 milliliters	=	3 tablespoons
1¾ fluid ounces	=	50 milliliters	=	3½ tablespoons
2 ounces	=	60 milliliters	=	4 tablespoons

Granulated Sugar

¼ cup	=	50 grams
⅓ cup	=	67 grams
½ cup	=	100 grams
⅔ cup	=	134 grams
¾ cup	=	150 grams
1 cup	=	200 grams

DIY HOMEMADE INGREDIENTS & STOCKING YOUR BAR

THE SWEETER THINGS IN LIFE

Sweeteners are an integral part of creating a balanced drink, and they come in many forms and styles, from the most basic simple syrup to the slightly more complex oleo-saccharum (see page 31). Choosing the right sweetener for your drink can drastically change how the drink tastes and feels on your palate. Honey syrups provide not only flavor but a distinct mouthfeel in comparison to traditional sugar syrups. Don't think of sweeteners as an afterthought. Think of them as another opportunity to get creative!

THE BASICS

These are the syrups you will see the most throughout the book. They are easily made in just a few steps with basic kitchen equipment. The recipes are listed in volume measurements; if you prefer to use by weight, follow the grams conversions. Increase or decrease the measurements to make the syrups in small or large batches. Remember to store all homemade syrups in the refrigerator in an airtight container.

AGAVE SYRUP
(2:1 BY VOLUME)

Makes 12 fluid ounces

8 fluid ounces (350g) amber agave nectar

4 fluid ounces (120g) filtered water

In a medium saucepan, combine the agave nectar and filtered water and heat over medium heat, stirring until the agave nectar has fully dissolved. Let cool, then bottle and store in the fridge for up to 1 month.

DEMERARA SYRUP
(2:1 BY VOLUME AND WEIGHT)

Makes 12 fluid ounces

1½ cups (350g) demerara sugar

6 fluid ounces (180g) filtered water

In a medium saucepan, combine the demerara sugar and water and heat over medium heat, stirring continuously, until the sugar has fully dissolved. Let cool, then bottle and store in the fridge for up to 1 month.

SIMPLE SYRUP
(1:1 BY VOLUME AND WEIGHT)

Makes 12 fluid ounces

1 cup (200g) granulated sugar
8 fluid ounces (240g) filtered water

In a medium saucepan, combine the sugar and water and heat over medium heat, stirring until the sugar has fully dissolved. Let cool, then bottle and store in the fridge for up to 1 month.

RICH SIMPLE SYRUP
(2:1 BY VOLUME AND WEIGHT)

Makes 16 fluid ounces

2 cups (400g) granulated sugar
8 fluid ounces (240g) filtered water

In a medium saucepan, combine the sugar and water and heat over medium heat, stirring until sugar has fully dissolved. Let cool, then bottle and store in the fridge for up to 1 month.

BLACKBERRY SYRUP
(1:1 BY VOLUME AND WEIGHT)

Makes 14 fluid ounces

1 cup (200g) granulated sugar
8 fluid ounces (240g) filtered water
½ cup blackberries, fresh or frozen

In a medium saucepan, combine the sugar, water, and blackberries and heat over medium heat, stirring until the sugar has fully dissolved. Using a potato masher or muddler, break up the blackberries. Cook for an additional 3 minutes. After cooling, use a fine-mesh sieve to strain out the seeds and pulp. Bottle and store in the fridge for up to a month.

CINNAMON SYRUP
(1:1 BY VOLUME AND WEIGHT)

Makes 12 fluid ounces

1 cinnamon stick
1 cup (200g) granulated sugar
8 fluid ounces (240g) filtered water

Add the cinnamon stick to a medium saucepan. Gently break up the cinnamon stick with a mallet or muddler. Heat over low heat for 30 seconds or until fragrant. Add the sugar and filtered water, then turn the heat up to medium and stir until the sugar has fully dissolved. After cooling, use a fine-mesh sieve to strain out the cinnamon stick. Bottle and store in the fridge for up to 1 month.

JALAPEÑO SYRUP
(1:1 BY VOLUME AND WEIGHT)

Makes 12 fluid ounces

1 cup (200g) granulated sugar
8 fluid ounces (240g) filtered water
1½ teaspoons chopped jalapeño
¼ teaspoon kosher salt

In a medium saucepan, combine the sugar, water, and jalapeño and heat over medium heat, stirring until the sugar has fully dissolved. After cooling, use a fine-mesh sieve to strain out the jalapeño. Bottle and store in the fridge for up to 1 month.

RASPBERRY SYRUP
(1:1 BY VOLUME AND WEIGHT)

Makes 14 fluid ounces

1 cup (200g) granulated sugar
8 fluid ounces (240g) filtered water
½ cup raspberries, fresh or frozen

In a medium saucepan, combine the sugar, water, and raspberries and heat over medium heat, stirring until the sugar has fully dissolved. Using a potato masher or muddler, break up the raspberries. Cook for an additional 3 minutes. After cooling, use a fine-mesh sieve to strain out the raspberry seeds and pulp. Bottle and store in the fridge for up to 1 month.

ROSEMARY SYRUP
(1:1 BY VOLUME AND WEIGHT)

Makes 12 fluid ounces

1 cup (200g) granulated sugar
8 fluid ounces (240g) filtered water
2 sprigs rosemary

In a medium saucepan, combine the sugar, water, and rosemary and heat over medium heat, stirring until the sugar has fully dissolved. After cooling, use a fine-mesh sieve to strain out the rosemary sprigs. Bottle and store in the fridge for up to 1 month.

VANILLA BEAN SYRUP
(1:1 BY VOLUME AND WEIGHT)

Makes 12 ounces

1 cup (200g) granulated sugar
8 fluid ounces (240g) filtered water
1 vanilla bean

In a medium saucepan, combine the sugar and water. Split the vanilla bean lengthwise with a paring knife. Using the edge of the knife, scrape the seeds out of the pod and into the saucepan. Heat over medium heat, stirring until the sugar has fully dissolved. Let cool, then bottle and store in the fridge.

HONEY SYRUP
(2:1 BY VOLUME AND WEIGHT)

Makes 10 fluid ounces

6 fluid ounces (275g) liquid honey
4 fluid ounces (120g) filtered water

In a medium saucepan, combine the honey and water and heat over low heat, stirring until the honey and water have combined, about 2 minutes. Let cool, then bottle and store in the fridge for up to 2 months.

BLACK PEPPER HONEY SYRUP
(2:1 BY VOLUME AND WEIGHT)

Makes 10 fluid ounces

1½ teaspoons black peppercorns
6 fluid ounces (275g) liquid honey
4 fluid ounces (120g) filtered water

Add the black peppercorns to a medium saucepan and gently break them up with a mallet or muddler. Heat the peppercorns over low heat for 30 seconds or until fragrant. Add the honey and water, turning the heat up to medium, stirring until the honey and water have combined, about 2 minutes. After cooling, use a fine-mesh sieve to strain out the peppercorns. Bottle and store in the fridge for up to 2 months.

GINGER HONEY SYRUP
(2:1 BY VOLUME AND WEIGHT)

Makes 10 fluid ounces

6 fluid ounces (275g) liquid honey
4 fluid ounces (120g) filtered water
1 tablespoon grated fresh ginger

In a medium saucepan, combine the honey, water, and ginger and heat over medium-low heat, stirring until the honey and water have combined, about 2 minutes. After cooling, using a fine-mesh sieve to strain out the ginger. Bottle and store in the fridge for up to 2 months.

GINGER & LAVENDER HONEY SYRUP
(2:1 BY VOLUME AND WEIGHT)

Makes 10 fluid ounces

6 fluid ounces (275g) liquid honey
4 fluid ounces (120g) filtered water
1 tablespoon grated fresh ginger
1 tablespoon dried lavender
¼ teaspoon table salt

In a medium saucepan, combine the honey, water, ginger, lavender, and salt and heat over medium-low heat, stirring until the honey and water have combined, about 2 minutes. After cooling, use a fine-mesh sieve to strain out the ginger and lavender. Bottle and store in the fridge for up to 2 months.

SPICED HONEY SYRUP
(2:1 BY VOLUME AND WEIGHT)

Makes 10 fluid ounces

1 cinnamon stick

1 whole star anise

4 whole cloves

4 allspice berries

6 fluid ounces (275g) liquid honey

4 fluid ounces (120g) filtered water

In a medium saucepan, combine the cinnamon stick, star anise, cloves, and allspice. Gently break up the spices with a mallet or muddler. Heat over low heat for 30 seconds, or until fragrant. Add the honey and water, turning the heat up to medium, stirring until the honey and water have combined, about 2 minutes. After cooling, use a fine-mesh sieve to strain out the spices. Bottle and store in the fridge for up to 2 months.

INTERMEDIATE SYRUPS

These syrups require a bit more time and attention. Still easily made at home with basic kitchen equipment, but with a few ingredients you will likely need to source. Once you have these recipes nailed down, you'll never go back to buying store-bought mixers.

PINEAPPLE GOMME SYRUP
(2:1 BY VOLUME AND WEIGHT)

Makes 18 fluid ounces

2 fluid ounces (60g) hot water

1½ teaspoons (8g) gum arabic powder

2 cups (400g) granulated sugar

8 fluid ounces (240g) filtered water

1 cup pineapple chunks

1 fluid ounce (30g) pineapple juice

Add the hot water to a heatproof bowl. Slowly add the gum arabic powder and whisk vigorously, making sure to break up all the clumps. Set aside.

In a medium saucepan, combine the sugar, water, pineapple chunks, and pineapple juice and heat over medium heat, stirring until the sugar has fully dissolved. Bring to a boil and immediately remove from the heat. After cooling, use a fine-mesh sieve to strain out the pineapple chunks. Add the gum arabic mixture to the pineapple syrup and stir to combine. Bottle and store in the fridge for up to 1 month.

FALERNUM

12 fluid ounces (350g) filtered water

1 teaspoon whole cloves

1½ tablespoons grated fresh ginger

1 cinnamon stick

1 whole star anise

Grated zest of 2 limes

2 cups (400g) granulated sugar

4 fluid ounces (120g) overproof rum (optional; see Note)

In a blender, combine the water, cloves, ginger, cinnamon stick, star anise, and lime zest and pulse to combine. Pour the mixture into a medium saucepan. Add the sugar and stir over medium heat until fully dissolved. Bring to a boil and reduce the heat to low and let simmer for 15 minutes. After cooling, use a fine-mesh sieve to strain out the spices and zest. Add the rum, if using, to the syrup. Bottle and store in the fridge. The syrup will keep for 1 month without the rum and up to 3 months with the rum.

Note: Traditionally, falernum contains overproof rum. You can omit the rum to keep it nonalcoholic.

ORGEAT

2 cups (184g) raw almonds, sliced or chopped

1½ cups (300g) granulated sugar

10 fluid ounces (270g) filtered water

1 teaspoon orange blossom water

1 ounce vodka (optional)

Preheat the oven to 400°F.

Spread the almonds on a baking sheet and roast for 4 minutes, shaking the pan after 2 minutes. Cool the almonds and then pulverize in a food processor or blender.

In a medium saucepan, combine the sugar and water and stir over medium heat until the sugar has fully dissolved. Add the pulverized almonds and simmer over low heat for 10 minutes, stirring frequently.

After cooling, use fine cheesecloth or a nut milk bag to strain the orgeat into a clean bowl. Add the orange blossom water and vodka (if using) and stir to incorporate. Bottle and store in the fridge. The orgeat will keep for 1 month without the vodka and up to 3 months with the vodka.

TOASTED SESAME MISO ORGEAT

⅓ cup toasted sesame seeds

1 cup (200g) granulated sugar

8 fluid ounces (240g) filtered water

1 tablespoon white miso paste

1 teaspoon orange blossom water

In a blender, combine the sesame seeds, sugar, water, and miso paste and blend on high for 1 minute. Transfer to a medium saucepan and bring to a simmer over medium-low heat. Continue simmering for 10 minutes, stirring frequently. After cooling, use fine cheesecloth or a nut milk bag to strain the orgeat into a clean bowl. Add the orange blossom water and stir to incorporate. Bottle and store in the fridge for 1 month.

OLEO–SACCHARUM

It sounds more complicated than it is. *Oleo-saccharum* is Latin for "oil-sugar," and it is a technique that has been used for centuries. Sugar is used to pull naturally occurring oils from citrus fruit, creating a lush oily sugar syrup that's perfect for adding more flavor to your favorite cocktail.

You can make an oleo-saccharum with just about any type of citrus. Below I give several recipe variations with ingredients and then a universal method for making any one of the oleo-saccharums.

Lemon Oleo-Saccharum

Makes 8 fluid ounces

6 lemons
1½ cups (300g) granulated sugar
4 fluid ounces (120g) fresh lemon juice

Grapefruit Oleo-Saccharum

Makes 8 fluid ounces

3 large grapefruits
1½ cups (300g) granulated sugar
4 fluid ounces (120g) fresh grapefruit juice

Orange Oleo-Saccharum

Makes 8 fluid ounces

4 navel oranges
1½ cups (300g) granulated sugar
4 ounces (120g) fresh orange juice

Earl Grey Oleo-Saccharum

Makes 10 fluid ounces

3 large grapefruits
2 cups (400g) granulated sugar
6 fluid ounces steeped Earl Grey tea

To make any of the oleo-saccharums:

Wash and peel the citrus fruit. Using a small paring knife, remove as much of the excess white pith from the peels. Place the peels in a sealable jar or container and cover with the sugar. Using a muddler, gently muddle the peels and sugar together. Seal the jar or container and leave out at room temperature overnight. The clear citrus oil syrup found floating at the top of your jar or container the next day is pure oleo-saccharum. To dissolve the sugar and make a syrup, add the citrus juice or steeped tea and mix well. Using a fine-mesh sieve, strain the oleo-saccharum into a bottle and store in the fridge for 1 month.

THE SOUR THINGS IN LIFE

Where there's sweet, there's sour. Continuing in the pursuit of the balanced cocktail, you can't leave out acidity. Acid counteracts sweetness, enhances aromatics, and can influence overall mouthfeel. When it comes to acidity, don't just limit yourself to the obvious, lemon and lime juice. There are many alternatives that can be used to achieve the same impact: vermouths, verjus, ferments, shrubs, and my favorite, alternative acids.

SHRUBS

A shrub, also known as a drinking vinegar, is a combination of vinegar, sugar, and fruit. It is often used as a replacement for citrus in cocktails to add more complexity and depth of flavor. It's also a great way to preserve seasonal fruit flavors you can use all year round.

CRANBERRY SHRUB

Makes 20 fluid ounces

2¼ cups cranberries, fresh or frozen

¾ cup (150g) granulated sugar

6 fluid ounces (180g) filtered water

1 cinnamon stick

8 fluid ounces (240g) apple cider vinegar

In a medium saucepan, combine the cranberries, sugar, water, and cinnamon stick and stir over medium heat until the sugar has fully dissolved. Bring to a boil, then reduce the heat to a simmer and cook until the cranberries are soft, about 8 minutes. After cooling, use a fine-mesh sieve to strain out the cranberries and cinnamon stick, pouring the syrup into a clean bowl. Add the apple cider vinegar and stir to incorporate. Bottle and store in the fridge for 2 months.

STRAWBERRY SHRUB

Makes 20 fluid ounces

2½ cups strawberries, fresh or frozen, chopped

¾ cup (150g) granulated sugar

6 fluid ounces (180g) filtered water

¼ teaspoon kosher salt

6 fluid ounces (180g) apple cider vinegar

2 fluid ounces (60g) balsamic vinegar

In a medium saucepan, combine the strawberries, sugar, water, and salt and stir over medium heat until the sugar has fully dissolved. Bring to a boil, then reduce to a simmer and cook until the strawberries are soft, about 6 minutes. After cooling, use a fine-mesh sieve to strain out the strawberries, pouring the syrup into a clean bowl. Add the apple cider vinegar and balsamic vinegar and stir to incorporate. Bottle and store in the fridge for 2 months.

ACID–ADJUSTED JUICES

The technique of acid-adjusting juices is really quite simple. You are essentially just increasing the acidity level of a fruit, or sometimes a vegetable, to provide the proper balance to a cocktail without changing its original flavor. For example, an orange is an acidic fruit, but it's not acidic enough to provide balance on its own. By increasing the acidity of the orange with additional acids—to the level of a lime or a lemon—you can then use the acidified orange juice for both flavor and acidic function. You can acidify pretty much anything that will juice. Below I give several recipe variations with ingredients and then a universal method for making any acidified juice used in the book.

Acidified Grapefruit Juice
(to the level of a lime)

34 fluid ounces (1.05kg) grapefruit juice
1 tablespoon plus ¾ teaspoon (25g) citric acid
2 teaspoons (18g) malic acid

Acidified Orange Juice
(to the level of a lime)

34 fluid ounces (1.05kg) orange juice
1½ tablespoons plus ¾ teaspoon (32g) citric acid
1 tablespoon (20g) malic acid

Acidified Pineapple Juice
(to the level of a lime)

34 fluid ounces (1.05kg) pineapple juice
1½ tablespoons plus ¾ teaspoon (32g) citric acid
1 tablespoon (20g) malic acid

Acidified Raspberry Juice
(to the level of a lime)

34 fluid ounces (1.05kg) raspberry juice
1½ tablespoons (27g) citric acid

Acidified Watermelon Juice
(to the level of a lime)

34 fluid ounces (1.05kg) watermelon juice
2 tablespoons (40g) citric acid
1½ teaspoons (10g) malic acid

Acid Blend (to the level of a lime)

34 fluid ounces (1.05g) filtered water
1½ tablespoons plus ¾ teaspoon (32g) citric acid
1½ tablespoons plus ¾ teaspoon (32g) malic acid
¼ teaspoon (3g) table salt

To make any of the acidified juices or blend:
Add the juice or water, alternative acids, and salt, if called for, to a clean container and mix until the acids have fully dissolved. Bottle and store in the fridge for 2 weeks.

INFUSIONS AND OTHER HOMEMADE INGREDIENTS

An easy way to add even more flavor to your favorite cocktail is to infuse the spirits that you use. This doesn't require any fancy equipment, just a bit of time and patience. The spirit you use is going to do all the hard work for you. Alcohol is a solvent and a master at extracting flavors. Here you will find the recipes for all the infused and homemade spirits you'll come across in this book. You can also use the instructions as a guide to start creating your own flavors at home. I like to use a French coffee press when infusing spirits. It already has a built-in press and strainer to make for easy execution and cleanup. Alternatively, you can use a mason jar and a fine-mesh sieve or fine cheesecloth.

BLACKBERRY TEQUILA

17 fluid ounces (500ml) blanco tequila

1 cup (145g) frozen blackberries

In a French press, combine the tequila and blackberries. Press down firmly and let sit at room temperature for 24 hours. Strain into a clean bottle and store in a cool dark place for 6 months.

BLUEBERRY ORANGE LIQUEUR

17 fluid ounces (500ml) orange liqueur

1 cup (145g) frozen blueberries

In a French press, combine the liqueur and blueberries. Press down firmly and let sit at room temperature for 24 hours. Strain into a clean bottle and store in a cool dark place for 6 months.

EARL GREY GIN

17 fluid ounces (500ml) London Dry Gin

1 tablespoon (4g) Earl Grey tea leaves

In a French press, combine the gin and Earl Grey tea leaves. Press down firmly and let sit at room temperature for 2 hours. Strain into a clean bottle and store in a cool dark place for 6 months.

RASPBERRY COGNAC

17 fluid ounces (500ml) Cognac
1 cup (145g) frozen raspberries

In a French press, combine the Cognac and raspberries. Press down firmly and let sit at room temperature for 24 hours. Strain into a clean bottle and store in a cool dark place for 6 months.

STRAWBERRY COGNAC

17 fluid ounces (500ml) Cognac
1 cup (145g) frozen strawberries, chopped

In a French press, combine the Cognac and strawberries. Press down firmly and let sit at room temperature for 24 hours. Strain into a clean bottle and store in a cool dark place for 6 months.

OTHER HOMEMADE ELEMENTS

CEDAR-SMOKED RYE

1 tablespoon (4g) cedar wood chips
17 fluid ounces (500ml) rye whiskey

Set the cedar chips on a heatproof surface. With a kitchen torch, flame the chips until actively smoking. Place a jar upside down over the smoking wood chips and let sit until the wood chips have stopped smoking. Pour rye into the jar and seal. Let sit for 20 minutes before using.

CEREAL MILK

17 fluid ounces (500ml) whole milk
1 cup (105g) dry cereal of your choice

In a jar, combine the milk and cereal and seal. Shake for 10 seconds and let sit for 45 minutes. Using a sieve, strain out the cereal and discard. Bottle the milk and store in the fridge for up to 5 days.

CLARIFIED ORANGE JUICE

17 fluid ounces (500ml) freshly squeezed orange juice, at room temperature

1ml (20 drops) Pectinex

2ml (40 drops) Kieselsol

2ml (40 drops) Chitosan

In a clean container, combine the orange juice, Pectinex, and 1 ml Kieselsol. Give a gentle stir to incorporate and let sit for 10 minutes. Add the Chitosan and remaining 1ml Kieselsol. Give a gentle stir to incorporate and let sit for 10 minutes. Slowly strain through a damp coffee filter into a clean container. Bottle and store in the fridge for up to 7 days.

COLD BREW COFFEE
(7:1 RATIO)

17 fluid ounces (500ml) filtered water

¾ cup (70g) coarsely ground coffee

In a pitcher, combine the water and coffee and give a gentle stir to incorporate. Let sit for 18 to 24 hours at room temperature or in the fridge. Strain through a damp coffee filter into a clean container. Bottle and store in the fridge for 2 weeks.

MILK LIQUEUR

17 fluid ounces (500ml) whole milk

17 fluid ounces (500ml) vodka

2 cups (400g) granulated cane sugar

1 lemon, quartered

1 orange, quartered

In a clean container, combine the milk, vodka, and sugar. Squeeze the juice from the lemon and orange quarters into the container and add the quarters as well. Give a good stir to incorporate. Cover the container with cheesecloth and leave at room temperature for 10 days, stirring once a day. Slowly strain through a damp coffee filter or tight-weave cheesecloth into a clean container. To ensure a crystal-clear finish, do not rush the straining process. You may need to filter the mix two or three times. Bottle and store in the fridge for up to 1 year.

PINEAPPLE KASU

17 fluid ounces (500ml) fresh pineapple juice

4 fluid ounces (120ml) sake kasu

In a blender, combine the pineapple juice and sake kasu and blend on high until smooth, about 3 minutes. Bottle and store in the fridge for 1 week.

SALINE SOLUTION

1 tablespoon (9g) Diamond Crystal kosher salt

8 fluid ounces (240g) filtered water

In a nonreactive container, combine the salt and filtered water. Stir until the salt has dissolved. Bottle and store in the fridge indefinitely. Pour a small amount into an atomizer or eyedropper for convenience.

TEPACHE

1 medium pineapple

34 fluid ounces (1 liter) filtered water

½ cup (110g) unrefined cane sugar such as piloncillo or brown sugar

½ lime

1 cinnamon stick

3 whole cloves

2 whole star anise

1 teaspoon grated nutmeg

Wash the pineapple and carefully remove the crown. Be sure to save the pineapple leaves to use as garnishes. With a large kitchen knife, cut off the rind and remove the core. Save the flesh for other uses.

In a large nonreactive container, preferably glass, combine the filtered water and sugar and stir until the sugar has dissolved. Squeeze in the lime juice. Add the pineapple rinds and core, cinnamon stick, cloves, star anise, and nutmeg. Cover the container with cheesecloth, securing it around the top. Let sit at room temperature for 48 hours, checking on it periodically for foam forming due to fermentation. Scoop excess foam out and discard.

After 48 hours, taste your tepache. It should taste slightly fermented. If not, re-cover your container and wait another 24 hours. When the tepache is ready, strain out the solids. Bottle and store in the fridge to prevent further fermentation and keep for up to 1 week.

BREWED TEAS

Teas are such a great way to not only add flavor to a drink but also bring in tannins. The tannins of most teas help clean the palate and contribute a complex dryness to the drink; black teas are highest in tannins while green, white, and herbal teas are on the lower end. You will notice the use of a lot of teas, especially when it comes to the zero-proof sips, in this book. With so many amazing teas to choose from, the flavor possibilities are endless. Just be sure to follow the brew instructions carefully. An oversteeped tea doesn't always equal more flavor. Oversteeping tends to make the tea bitter and too tannic.

Brewed Chamomile Tea

2 tablespoons (4g) chamomile tea
8 fluid ounces (240g) filtered water
Brew time: 10 minutes
Water temperature: 160°F

Brewed Lavender Tea

2 tablespoons (4g) herbal lavender tea
8 fluid ounces (240g) filtered water
Brew time: 10 minutes
Water temperature: 205°F

Brewed Peach Tea

2 tablespoons (4g) herbal peach tea
8 fluid ounces (240g) filtered water
Brew time: 5 minutes
Water temperature: 200°F

Brewed Jasmine Tea

2 tablespoons (4g) jasmine tea
8 fluid ounces (240g) filtered water
Brew time: 3 minutes
Water temperature: 185°F

Brewed Licorice Tea

2 tablespoons (4g) licorice root tea
8 fluid ounces (240g) filtered water
Brew time: 10 minutes
Water temperature: 200°F

Brewed Lapsang Souchong Tea

2 tablespoons (4g) lapsang souchong tea
8 fluid ounces (240g) filtered water
Brew time: 3 minutes
Water temperature: 203°F

Brewed Earl Grey Tea

2 tablespoons (4g) Earl Grey tea
8 fluid ounces (240g) filtered water
Brew time: 5 minutes
Water temperature: 208°F

Brewed Black Tea

2 tablespoons (4g) black tea
8 fluid ounces (240g) filtered water
Brew time: 5 minutes
Water temperature: 212°F

Brewed Assam Tea

2 tablespoons (4g) Assam tea
8 fluid ounces (240g) filtered water
Brew time: 3 minutes
Water temperature: 100°F

STOCKING YOUR BAR

My biggest piece of advice when it comes to stocking your home bar: Don't overcomplicate things. Choose your three favorite classic cocktails, make sure you have those spirits on hand, and build from there. You will soon come to find that a lot of classic cocktail recipes use the same ingredients, just in different proportions. I like to break down a basic bar setup into three categories: base spirits, modifiers, and lengtheners.

BASE SPIRITS

There are six key base spirits every home bartender should know: brandy, gin, rum, tequila, vodka, and whiskey. You don't necessarily need all six to start your home bar collection, but it is a good place to start.

Brandy

Brandy is found in many classic cocktails. It is a distillate traditionally made from grapes but can also be made from other fruits such as apples, apricots, cherries, and even peaches.

There are a few other spirits that also fall under the brandy category, such as Cognac, Armagnac, pisco, and grappa.

My favorite classic brandy cocktail would have to be the Sidecar (page 156).

Gin

Gin is one of the most versatile spirits. It is perfect for a stirred-down, booze-forward drink and also works wonderfully in a shaken, citrus-style drink. Gin can be made from any neutral grain and flavored with all sorts of botanicals. But in order for gin to be considered gin, it must be made with juniper berries.

There are many styles of gin, each with its own unique flavor profile: London Dry, Plymouth, Old Tom, Genever, and New American.

My favorite classic gin cocktail would have to be the Corpse Reviver No. 2 (page 78).

Rum

Rum was one of the first spirits to be mixed into drinks. It has a sweeter profile because it is distilled from some form of sugar, typically molasses or pure sugarcane. Rum is the base for a lot of tropical drinks and several hot cocktails. There are many types of rum to choose from: light, gold, dark, overproof, spiced, and even cachaça.

My favorite classic rum cocktail would have to be the Daiquiri (page 82).

Tequila

Tequila is one of the most tightly regulated spirits. It has to be made in one of Mexico's five authorized tequila regions. It is distilled from the fermented juices of the agave plant, which gives it an earthy, vegetal flavor. There are several styles of tequila that are defined by how long they have been aged: blanco, up to 60 days; reposado, 2 months to almost a year; añejo, 1 to 3 years; extra añejo, 3 years or longer. There are also several other agave spirits, such as mezcal, sotol, and raicilla, to name a few.

My favorite classic tequila cocktail would have to be a Margarita (page 127).

Vodka

Vodka is the most neutral of all the spirits and can be distilled from just about anything. Wheat, potatoes, corn, grapes, and even beets. Because vodka is so neutral, it is very versatile and can be mixed into just about any drink. Vodka is rarely ever aged and can be made anywhere in the world.

My favorite classic vodka cocktail would have to be a Cosmopolitan (page 81).

Whiskey

Whiskey or whisky, depending on where it is from, is another spirit that comes with a lot of rules and regulations. It is typically distilled from malted grains such as wheat, rye, corn, barley, or a combination. There are several categories of whiskey/whisky, such as bourbon, Canadian whisky, Irish whiskey, Japanese whisky, rye whiskey, Scotch whisky, Tennessee whiskey, and blended whiskey. Whiskey/whisky is enjoyed mixed in a cocktail and more often on its own.

My favorite classic whiskey cocktail would have to be a Kentucky Buck (page 115).

Bonus Bottle: Nonalcoholic Spirits

With the rise in popularity of nonalcoholic cocktails, it is always a good idea to stock at least one nonalcoholic spirit on your bar cart. I would suggest going with a spirit-free gin or spirit-free aperitif. A small gesture of inclusion goes a long way.

MODIFIERS

Modifiers are a cocktail's best friend. They can either soften or enhance the base spirit, as well as add depth of flavor and body to your cocktail. The number of modifiers available to us today are endless. Here is a short list of the most versatile modifiers to have on hand.

Aperitif/Digestif

APEROL
An infusion of bitter and sweet oranges, rhubarb, quinine, gentian, and many other botanicals.

CAMPARI
An infusion of chinotto, cascarilla, and other herbs and fruit.

AMARO MONTENEGRO
An infusion of forty botanicals including vanilla, orange peels, and eucalyptus.

FERNET-BRANCA
An infusion of more than forty herbs and spices including myrrh, rhubarb, chamomile, cardamom, and saffron.

CYNAR
An infusion of thirteen herbs and plants, the predominant one being artichoke.

Herbal/Spiced Liqueurs

GREEN CHARTREUSE/YELLOW CHARTREUSE
An infusion of 130 different plants, barks, roots, spices, and flowers. Green Chartreuse is made from a base of sugar-beet liquor, and yellow Chartreuse is made from a grape-based distillate.

STREGA
An infusion of seventy botanicals including saffron, mint, juniper berries, cinnamon, white pepper, cloves, and orris root.

ABSINTHE
A neutral spirit infused with botanicals such as anise, fennel, and wormwood.

ITALICUS
An infusion of Calabrian bergamot oranges, Sicilian citron, chamomile, lavender, yellow roses, lemon balm, and gentian.

Fortified Wines

LILLET

Made from a blend of Bordeaux grapes and fortified with fruit liqueurs, Lillet is further macerated with sweet, bitter, and green oranges and quinine. It is then aged in Yugoslav oak casks for one year.

VERMOUTH

There are several styles of vermouth, the most common being dry vermouth and sweet vermouth. They all have their own unique flavor profiles and can be infused with several different types of herbs and botanicals. But what they all must have in common is that they need to be made with at least 75 percent wine.

SHERRY

A fortified wine made from three key green grape varietals, Palomino, Moscatel, and Pedro Ximénez. They are aged in a solera system (a method of aging and blending liquids of many vintages) and can range from bone-dry to very sweet.

Fruit Liqueurs

ORANGE LIQUEUR

Made from either a neutral base spirit, rum, or brandy, orange liqueur is infused with sweet and bitter oranges.

ELDERFLOWER LIQUEUR

Typically made from a blend of Chardonnay and Gamay grapes, elderflower liqueur is infused with fresh elderflowers.

MARASCHINO LIQUEUR

An infusion of Marasca cherries and their pits gives Maraschino liqueur a slight almond flavor.

CASSIS

An infusion made from black currants.

AMARETTO

An infusion made from apricot kernels or sometimes almonds.

LENGTHENERS

Lengtheners, also commonly referred to as mixers, are used to do exactly as the name suggests, lengthen your drink. They provide a form of dilution, can be effervescent, and provide balance. Lengtheners can be both nonalcoholic and alcoholic.

Sparkling Wine

Champagne, Cava, prosecco, Lambrusco.

Tonic

A carbonated mixer that is infused with quinine and, in most cases, sugar.

Soda

Carbonated or sparkling water.

Ginger Beer

A fermented, sweetened, and carbonated beverage with an intense ginger kick.

BITTERS AND TINCTURES

Bitters are concentrated flavor extracts made by infusing herbs, barks, spices, roots, and other botanicals in high-proof alcohol or glycerin. Because the extracts are so concentrated, a little will go a long way. They are often referred to as the "salt and pepper" of the cocktail world. Bitters are a great way to enhance flavors in cocktails, temper sweetness, and add depth. Bitters were originally created for medicinal purposes. So the next time you have a stomachache or indigestion, try adding a couple of dashes of bitters to your soda water. Traditional bitters are alcohol-based, much like vanilla extract. However, there are plenty of nonalcoholic bitters options now available.

These are my staple bar cart bitters I always have on hand.

Angostura Bitters

An infusion of gentian, herbs, and spices.

Orange Bitters

An infusion of orange peels, herbs, and spices.

Peychaud's Bitters

An infusion of herbs and spices such as anise, clove, and gentian.

GLASSWARE

Every glass has a place and purpose. Yes, you can technically drink out of anything, but the style of glass you choose can affect the overall enjoyment of your cocktail.

Stemware such as martini, coupe, and wine glasses are designed to keep the warmth of your hand away from the drink itself. You hold these glasses by the stem so the cocktail can stay at its desired temperature for longer.

Rocks glasses are ideal for neat pours and drinks served over ice. Collins and highball glasses are perfect for drinks that are accompanied by a lengthener because of the volume they hold.

I suggest stocking your home bar with five key styles of glasses and then build from there.

Martini Glass

Some may say the martini glass is a bit outdated, but I like to believe that it is timeless. Used primarily for the classic martini made with gin or vodka, the martini glass has a wide mouth that allows you to take in air as you sip, helping to open up all of the botanicals in the vermouth and gin.

Coupe Glass

Originally used to serve Champagne, the coupe is now used for practically any cocktail served up (meaning a drink that is not served over ice). The coupe is recognized for its shallow bowl and stem. An alternative to the coupe is the Nick & Nora glass. Slightly smaller in capacity, these two glasses are often interchangeable.

Rocks Glass

Also referred to as an old-fashioned glass, the rocks glass is used for both neat pours as well as drinks served over ice. They vary in size and capacity and can be used to build a drink directly inside, such as a Negroni.

Collins/Highball Glass

A tall and slender drinking vessel that is most commonly used for drinks that require a lengthener such as soda or tonic water. The collins glass tends to have a slightly bigger capacity than the highball glass, but their general purpose is the same.

Wine Glass/Flute

Apart from the obvious, a wine glass is the perfect go-between glass of the coupe, rocks, and collins glass. It can handle ice, has a stem, and typically holds a lot of volume. A wine glass is perfect for a spritz, gin and tonic, and of course wine. The flute is the preferred glassware for sparkling wine due to its cone-like shape and tapered lip that helps retain carbonation. Drinks like the Air Mail and French 75 thrive in a flute.

LIKE·A·BLE

COCKTAILS

FOR EVERYONE

AT EVERY PROOF

CLASSIC COCKTAIL LIST A TO Z

Left to right: Return to Sender, Air Mail, Pen Pal

AIR MAIL

1940s
Each recipe makes 1 cocktail

"It ought to make you fly high."
—W. C. Whitfield

And indeed it will make you fly high. Often referred to as a rum-based French 75, this light, bright, and refreshing bubbly cocktail will sneak up on you. Perfect for brunch or as an aperitif, the Air Mail, which first appeared in print in 1941 in W. C. Whitfield's *Here's How,* is easy to make and even easier to drink. If you're looking to be a bit more adventurous, give the Pen Pal a try, which subs in tequila and Aperol to give this drink even more depth of flavor while still keeping things light and bright. If you want to avoid the booze altogether, then the Return to Sender is for you.

CLASSIC **AIR MAIL**	RIFF **PEN PAL**	N–A **RETURN TO SENDER**
GLASSWARE highball	**GLASSWARE** highball	**GLASSWARE** highball
1 ounce gold rum ½ ounce fresh lime juice ½ ounce Honey Syrup (page 28) 2 ounces Champagne or sparkling wine Mint sprig, for garnish	1 ounce blanco tequila ½ ounce Aperol ¾ ounce fresh lemon juice ½ ounce Rich Simple Syrup (page 26) 2 dashes Peychaud's bitters 2 ounces Champagne or sparkling wine Grapefruit twist, for garnish	1 ounce spirit-free rum ½ ounce fresh lemon juice ½ ounce Spiced Honey Syrup (page 29) 3 fresh mint leaves 4 ounces nonalcoholic sparkling wine Mint sprig, for garnish
In a shaker tin, combine the rum, lime juice, and honey syrup. Add cubed ice and shake vigorously for 7 seconds. Fine-strain into an ice-filled highball glass and top with Champagne. Gently stir to incorporate and garnish with a sprig of mint.	In a shaker tin, combine the tequila, Aperol, lemon juice, rich simple syrup, and bitters. Add cubed ice and shake vigorously for 7 seconds. Fine-strain into an ice-filled highball glass and top with Champagne. Gently stir to incorporate and garnish with a grapefruit twist.	In a shaker tin, combine the spirit-free rum, lemon juice, spiced honey syrup, and mint leaves. Add cubed ice and shake vigorously for 7 seconds. Fine-strain into an ice-filled highball glass and top with nonalcoholic sparkling wine. Gently stir to incorporate and garnish with a mint sprig.

 PRO TIP Always gently stir your drink after adding in any sort of mixer. This will ensure that when you take your first sip, you are experiencing the entire drink and not just the last ingredient you added.

APERITIF SPRITZ

19th Century
Each recipe makes 1 cocktail

The spritz comes to us from Northern Italy, in the Veneto region where prosecco comes from, and is as easy as 1-2-3: one part aperitif, two parts soda water, and three parts prosecco. The spritz originated in the 1800s when Austrians who were visiting Italy would add a splash or "spritz" of soda water to the local wines to make them lighter. Keeping the 1-2-3 formula in mind, "choose your own adventure" and swap in whatever aperitif you like! Amaro, vermouth, and sherry all make excellent spritz-style cocktails. Add a shot of gin or a squeeze of citrus for an even better spritz experience. The Jingle T*ts Spritz has quickly become a holiday favorite, for no other reason than once you start drinking them it's hard to stop and they'll have you jingling your t*ts all night long.

CLASSIC APERITIF SPRITZ	RIFF JINGLE T*TS SPRITZ	N—A FEELIN' SPRITZY
GLASSWARE wine	**GLASSWARE** wine	**GLASSWARE** wine
1 ounce Aperol 2 ounces soda water 3 ounces prosecco Orange slice and green olive, for garnish	¾ ounce gin ½ ounce Aperol 1 ounce fresh mandarin orange juice ½ ounce fresh lemon juice ½ ounce Simple Syrup (page 26) 2 ounces dry sparkling wine (cava or brut) Orange slice, for garnish	1 ounce Wilfred's nonalcoholic aperitif ¾ ounce grapefruit juice 1 ounce soda water 3 ounces nonalcoholic sparkling wine Grapefruit wedge and rosemary sprig, for garnish
Add the Aperol to a wine glass. Fill the glass with cubed ice and top with soda water and prosecco. Gently stir to incorporate and garnish with an orange slice and green olive.	In a shaker tin, combine the gin, Aperol, orange juice, lemon juice, and simple syrup. Add cubed ice and shake vigorously for 7 seconds. Fine-strain into an ice-filled wine glass and top with sparkling wine. Gently stir to incorporate and garnish with an orange slice.	In a wine glass, combine the nonalcoholic aperitif and grapefruit juice. Fill the glass with cubed ice and top with soda water and nonalcoholic sparkling wine. Gently stir to incorporate and garnish with a grapefruit wedge and rosemary sprig.

PRO TIP If you find prosecco too sweet, swap it out with a drier sparkling wine like cava.

Left to right: Jingle T*ts Spritz, Aperitif Spritz, Feelin' Spritzy

Left to right: Bee's Knees,
Cat's Meow, Tiger's Spots

BEE'S KNEES

1920s
Each recipe makes 1 cocktail

Said to be created by Austrian-born bartender Frank Meier in the 1920s, this cocktail is a simple extension of the classic gin sour. It follows the basic template of using spirit, sugar, and citrus. It got its unique name from the once-popular phrase "bee's knees," which was used to refer to something as excellent or outstanding, as in, "It's the bee's knees!" This cocktail most certainly is! Because of the simplicity of this drink, it is an easy one to play around with. Use a flavored honey syrup or split the base spirit as I've done in the Cat's Meow. A good cocktail doesn't always have to be a complicated cocktail.

CLASSIC BEE'S KNEES	RIFF CAT'S MEOW	N—A TIGER'S SPOTS
GLASSWARE chilled coupe	**GLASSWARE** chilled coupe	**GLASSWARE** chilled coupe
2 ounces gin ½ ounce Honey Syrup (page 28) ¾ ounce fresh lemon juice Lemon twist, for garnish	1 ounce gin 1 ounce Cognac ¾ ounce Ginger & Lavender Honey Syrup (page 28) 1 ounce fresh lemon juice 3 drops Saline Solution (page 40) Lemon coin, for garnish	2 lemon wedges 2 ounces spirit-free gin ¾ ounce Ginger & Lavender Honey Syrup (page 28) 3 drops Saline Solution (page 40) Lemon coin, for garnish
In a shaker tin, combine the gin, honey syrup, and lemon juice. Add cubed ice and shake vigorously for 12 seconds. Fine-strain into a chilled coupe glass and garnish with the lemon twist.	In a shaker tin, combine the gin, Cognac, honey syrup, lemon juice, and saline solution. Add cubed ice and shake vigorously for 12 seconds. Fine-strain into a chilled coupe glass and garnish with the lemon coin.	Add the 2 lemon wedges to a shaker tin. Gently muddle to release the juice and express the oils from the peels. Add the spirit-free gin, ginger & lavender honey syrup, and saline solution and fill with cubed ice. Shake vigorously for 10 seconds. Fine-strain into a chilled coupe glass and garnish with a lemon coin.

PRO TIP Honey syrup can be fairly sticky. It is always good practice to measure it out first so that the ingredients to follow will help "rinse" out your jigger.

BICYCLE THIEF

2010s
Each recipes makes 1 cocktail

Here's a slightly bitter thirst quencher from New York City's Dutch Kills bar. The combination of Campari and grapefruit make for an approachable drink that even the Campari skeptic will enjoy. Still not convinced? Then try your hand at the Bicicletta for an Aperol variation—not quite as bitter but still extremely quenching. Want the bitterness without the buzz? Then the Tricycle is just the drink for you. Plus it has a scoop of lemon sorbet. Winning!

CLASSIC BICYCLE THIEF	RIFF BICICLETTA	N—A TRICYCLE
GLASSWARE highball	GLASSWARE rocks	GLASSWARE rocks
1 ounce gin 1 ounce Campari 1½ ounces grapefruit juice ½ ounce fresh lemon juice ½ ounce Simple Syrup (page 26) 1½ ounces soda water Grapefruit slice, for garnish	1 ounce gin ½ ounce Italicus bergamot liqueur ½ ounce Aperol 1½ ounces grapefruit juice ½ ounce fresh lime juice ½ ounce Simple Syrup (page 26) Grapefruit slice, for garnish	1 ounce spirit-free gin 1 ounce grapefruit juice 1 bottle Stappi Red Bitter soda 1 scoop lemon sorbet Grapefruit twist, for garnish
In a shaker tin, combine the gin, Campari, grapefruit juice, lemon juice, and simple syrup. Add cubed ice and shake vigorously for 7 seconds. Fine-strain into a highball glass over fresh ice and top with soda water. Gently stir to incorporate and garnish with a grapefruit slice.	In a shaker tin, combine the gin, Italicus, Aperol, grapefruit juice, lime juice, and simple syrup. Add cubed ice and shake vigorously for 12 seconds. Fine-strain into a rocks glass over fresh ice and garnish with a grapefruit slice.	Combine the spirit-free gin, grapefruit juice, and Stappi Red Bitter soda in a rocks glass over a large piece of ice. Gently stir to incorporate. Add a scoop of lemon sorbet to sit on top of the ice and garnish with a grapefruit twist.

PRO TIP   If you are unable to consume grapefruit juice, use Acidified Orange Juice (page 34) as a replacement.

Left to right: Bicycle Thief, Tricycle, Bicicletta

Left to right: Bramble, Prickly Peach, Shrub a Dub Dub

BRAMBLE

1984
Each recipe makes 1 cocktail

You would think this drink was centuries old, but the bramble is an '80s classic. Created by Dick Bradsell, the Bramble is a riff on a classic gin sour with the addition of a blackberry liqueur. It is tart and fresh, perfect for sipping on a hot day. Play around with the original recipe to really make it your own. Swap out that blackberry liqueur for Chambord or cassis. Or use the fruit of whatever season you are in. Peaches and strawberries provide a familiar yet bold flavor to the modern twist and zero-proof sip.

CLASSIC BRAMBLE	RIFF PRICKLY PEACH	N-A SHRUB A DUB DUB
GLASSWARE rocks	**GLASSWARE** rocks	**GLASSWARE** rocks
2 ounces gin 1 ounce fresh lemon juice ½ ounce Simple Syrup (page 26) ½ ounce crème de mûre (blackberry liqueur) Fresh blackberry, for garnish	2 ounces pisco ¾ ounce fresh lime juice ½ ounce Simple Syrup (page 26) ½ ounce peach liqueur 2 dashes Angostura bitters Peach slice, for garnish	1½ ounces strongly Brewed Chamomile Tea (page 41) 1 ounce Strawberry Shrub (page 33) ½ ounce Simple Syrup (page 26) 2 whole strawberries Strawberry slice and mint sprig, for garnish
In a shaker tin, combine the gin, lemon juice, and simple syrup. Add cubed ice and shake vigorously for 12 seconds. Strain into a rocks glass over cracked ice and carefully drizzle the blackberry liqueur on top. Garnish with a fresh blackberry.	In a shaker tin, combine the pisco, lime juice, and simple syrup. Add cubed ice and shake vigorously for 12 seconds. Strain into a rocks glass over cracked ice and carefully drizzle the peach liqueur on top. Garnish with the Angostura bitters and a fresh peach slice.	In a shaker tin, combine the chamomile tea, strawberry shrub, simple syrup, and whole strawberries. Gently muddle the strawberries. Add cubed ice and shake vigorously for 7 seconds. Fine-strain into a rocks glass over cracked ice. Garnish with a strawberry slice and mint sprig.

PRO TIP Using fresh, seasonal berries is always ideal. However, if fresh ones are unavailable, frozen fruit is perfectly acceptable. Just make sure to thaw them first.

CANTARITO

1970s
Each recipe makes 4 cocktails

The cantarito is very similar to the Paloma (page 140), with even more of a fresh citrus kick. The drink is named after the clay cup in which it is traditionally served in Jalisco, Mexico, where daytime temperatures can get extremely high. The clay cup keeps the drink insulated and the alkalinity of the unglazed clay neutralizes the acid from the citrus juice, balancing out the drink's flavors. Cantaritos are often sold at roadside stands, so the clay cup was often thrown to the ground when empty and left to become part of the earth once again. This is a great cocktail to make in a larger batch and store in the fridge at the ready.

CLASSIC CANTARITO	RIFF CLARIFIED CANTARITO	N—A CLAY POT PUNCH
GLASSWARE 4 clay cups (or collins)	**GLASSWARE** 4 rocks glasses	**GLASSWARE** 4 clay cups (or collins)
Lime wedge and Tajín, for the rims 8 ounces reposado tequila 3 ounces fresh grapefruit juice 3 ounces fresh orange juice 2 ounces fresh lime juice Pinch of salt 10 ounces grapefruit soda Lime wedges, for garnish	8 ounces reposado tequila 2 ounces Aperol 3 ounces fresh grapefruit juice 3 ounces fresh orange juice 2 ounces fresh lime juice 4 ounces whole milk 4 ounces grapefruit soda Chili candy, for garnish	8 ounces Brewed Peach Tea (page 41) 4 ounces fresh grapefruit juice 4 ounces fresh tangerine juice 2 ounces fresh lemon juice 2 ounces Lemon Oleo-Saccharum (page 31) 8 ounces lemon-lime soda Grapefruit slices and lemon slices, for garnish
Using a wedge of lime, rim the outside of your clay cup and roll in Tajín. In a shaker tin, combine the tequila, grapefruit juice, orange juice, lime juice, and salt. Add cubed ice and shake vigorously for 7 seconds. Strain into your rimmed clay cup over fresh ice and top with grapefruit soda. Garnish with a lime wedge.	In a large container, combine the tequila, Aperol, grapefruit juice, orange juice, and lime juice. In a medium saucepan, heat the milk over medium-low heat. Once the milk has come to a simmer, remove from the heat and combine with the cantarito base. Do not stir. Place the cantarito mix, uncovered, in the fridge and let sit for 3 to 4 hours (or longer). The mix should naturally separate.	In an ice-filled pitcher, combine the peach tea, grapefruit juice, tangerine juice, lemon juice, and lemon oleo-saccharum. Gently stir to incorporate. Pour 5 ounces of punch into each cup over ice and top each with 2 ounces lemon-lime soda. Garnish with a grapefruit and lemon slice.

Once the cantarito mix has settled, carefully and slowly strain through a coffee filter or tight-weave cheesecloth into a clean container until the mix is clear. To ensure a crystal-clear finish, do not rush the straining process. You may need to filter the mix two or three times.

Bottle and refrigerate until ready to serve.

Pour 4 ounces of the cantarito mix into each rocks glass over fresh ice and top each with 1 ounce grapefruit soda. Gently stir to incorporate and garnish with a piece of chili candy.

 PRO TIP Instead of using a lime wedge to rim your clay cup, try using chamoy (a Mexican sauce made of dried chiles, lime juice, and fruits) for an even more authentic Mexican drinking experience.

Left: Cantarito, *bottom right:* Clarified Cantarito, *top right:* Clay Pot Punch

Left to right: Tangerine Twist,
Chartreuse Swizzle, Canary Swizzle

CHARTREUSE SWIZZLE

2002
Each recipe makes 1 cocktail

Originating at Tres Agaves in San Francisco from bartender Marco Dionysos, this swizzle swaps out the traditional rum for the herbal liqueur, green Chartreuse. On paper it might not seem like the most obvious of flavor pairings, but the sweet and tangy taste of pineapple and warm baking spices of falernum tame the herbal kick from the green Chartreuse and come together harmoniously. The swizzle itself is a style of drink similar to a sour or rum punch, but it must be churned with a swizzle stick and is always served on crushed or pebble ice. The Canary Swizzle utilizes yellow instead of green chartreuse, which is slightly less herbal and a touch more sweet.

CLASSIC CHARTREUSE SWIZZLE	RIFF CANARY SWIZZLE	N—A TANGERINE TWIST
GLASSWARE collins	GLASSWARE collins	GLASSWARE collins
1½ ounces green Chartreuse 1 ounce pineapple juice ¾ ounce fresh lime juice ½ ounce Falernum (page 30) Mint sprig and grated nutmeg, for garnish	1 ounce rhum agricole ½ ounce yellow Chartreuse ½ ounce passion fruit liqueur ¾ ounce fresh lime juice ½ ounce Orgeat (page 30) Mint sprig and grated nutmeg, for garnish	2 ounces strongly Brewed Licorice Tea (page 41) 1 ounce fresh tangerine juice ½ ounce fresh lemon juice ½ ounce Orgeat (page 30) Tangerine slice and grated nutmeg, for garnish
In a collins glass, combine the green Chartreuse, pineapple juice, lime juice, and falernum. Add pebble ice to fill half the glass. With a swizzle stick or bar spoon, "swizzle" the mix and ice together (see Pro Tip) for 5 seconds. Add more pebble ice to fill the remainder of the glass. Swizzle again for another 5 seconds. Remove the swizzle stick and top the glass with more pebble ice. Garnish with a mint sprig and grated nutmeg.	In a collins glass, combine the rhum agricole, yellow Chartreuse, passion fruit liqueur, lime juice, and orgeat. Add pebble ice to fill half the glass. With a swizzle stick or bar spoon, "swizzle" the mix and ice together (see Pro Tip) for 5 seconds. Add more pebble ice to fill the remainder of the glass. Swizzle again for another 5 seconds. Remove the swizzle stick and top the glass with more pebble ice. Garnish with a mint sprig and grated nutmeg.	In a shaker tin, combine the licorice tea, tangerine juice, lemon juice, and orgeat. Add cubed ice and shake vigorously for 7 seconds. Fine-strain into a collins glass over pebble ice. Garnish with a tangerine slice and grated nutmeg.

PRO TIP When using a swizzle stick, it is best to place it between the palms of both hands and roll it in a continuous back-and-forth motion.

CLOVER CLUB

1890s
Each recipe makes 1 cocktail

The Clover Club is arguably Philadelphia's biggest claim to fame when it comes to classic cocktails. It is said to have first been served at the Bellevue-Stratford Hotel, which just so happened to be a very popular hangout among the upperclass men of Philly. Lawyers, doctors, and writers would all meet at the hotel and talk about the day's events all while sipping on this pink drink—because real men drink pink drinks! In all three variations, the raspberry is the main flavor focus. If you don't have raspberry syrup or juice, muddle fresh raspberries in their place.

CLASSIC CLOVER CLUB	RIFF CRIMSON CLOVER COLLINS	N—A MEMBERS ONLY
GLASSWARE chilled coupe	**GLASSWARE** collins	**GLASSWARE** flute
2 ounces gin ½ ounce dry vermouth ¾ ounce fresh lemon juice ¾ ounce Raspberry Syrup (page 27) 1 egg white (or 2 dashes of a vegan foamer) Fresh raspberry, for garnish	1½ ounces gin ½ ounce fino sherry ¾ ounce Acidified Raspberry Juice (page 34) ½ ounce Simple Syrup (page 26) 3 ounces soda water Fresh raspberry, for garnish	2 ounces spirit-free gin ¾ ounce Acidified Raspberry Juice (page 34) ½ ounce Rich Simple Syrup (page 26) 2 dashes orange bitters 2 ounces nonalcoholic sparkling wine Fresh raspberry, for garnish
In a shaker tin, combine the gin, dry vermouth, lemon juice, raspberry syrup, and egg white. Dry shake (without ice) vigorously for 10 seconds. Open the shaker tin, add cubed ice, and shake again for another 12 seconds. Fine-strain into a chilled coupe glass. Garnish with a fresh raspberry.	In a shaker tin, combine the gin, fino sherry, acidified raspberry juice, and simple syrup. Add cubed ice and shake vigorously for 7 seconds. Fine-strain into a collins glass over fresh ice and top with soda water. Garnish with a fresh raspberry.	In a shaker tin, combine the spirit-free gin, acidified raspberry juice, rich simple syrup, and orange bitters. Add cubed ice and shake vigorously for 7 seconds. Fine-strain into a Champagne flute and top with nonalcoholic sparkling wine. Garnish with a fresh raspberry.

PRO TIP Instead of dry shaking egg white cocktails, use a milk frother to add air to the egg whites. This will make them light and fluffy without the mess.

Left to right: Clover Club, Crimson Clover Collins, Members Only

Left to right: Oil Change, Corn 'n' Oil

CORN 'N' OIL

1700s
Each recipe makes 1 cocktail

The Corn 'n' Oil is complex in flavor but not in execution. It originated in the Caribbean, likely Barbados, and contains neither corn nor oil. You don't need any fancy equipment to put this drink together, just quality ingredients. The Corn 'n' Oil was traditionally made with molasses blackstrap rum and an island falernum, which gives the drink an oily-looking finish—hence the name. It's the perfect, uncomplicated tiki drink. For the modern twist, I opted to use cachaça, which is a Brazilian-style "rum" made from sugarcane. Its fermented funky finish gives the twisted version even more depth of flavor.

CLASSIC CORN 'N' OIL	RIFF OIL SLICK	N—A OIL CHANGE
GLASSWARE rocks	**GLASSWARE** rocks	**GLASSWARE** collins
2 ounces blackstrap rum ½ ounce Falernum (page 30; see Pro Tip) ½ ounce fresh lime juice 3 dashes Angostura bitters Lime wheel, for garnish	1 ounce cachaça 1 ounce aged rum ½ ounce Orgeat (page 30) ¼ ounce vanilla liqueur ¼ ounce ginger liqueur ¾ ounce fresh lime juice 2 dashes Angostura bitters Lime wheel and grated nutmeg, for garnish	2 ounces spirit-free rum ¾ ounce Ginger Honey Syrup (page 28) 3 drops sesame oil ¾ ounce fresh lime juice 2 ounces ginger beer Candied ginger and grated nutmeg, for garnish
In a rocks glass, combine the blackstrap rum, falernum, lime juice, and Angostura bitters. Add pebble ice and vigorously mix. Top the glass with more pebble ice and garnish with a lime wheel.	In a shaker tin, combine the cachaça, aged rum, orgeat, vanilla liqueur, ginger liqueur, lime juice, and Angostura bitters. Add cubed ice and shake vigorously for 12 seconds. Fine-strain into a rocks glass over pebble ice. Garnish with a lime wheel and grated nutmeg.	In a shaker tin, combine the spirit-free rum, ginger honey syrup, sesame oil, and lime juice. Add cubed ice and shake vigorously for 10 seconds. Fine-strain into a collins class and top with ginger beer. Garnish with candied ginger and grated nutmeg.

PRO TIP Feel free to use store-bought falernum if you don't want to make your own. It comes in both nonalcoholic and alcoholic versions, so be sure to check the label.

CORPSE REVIVER NO. 2

1870s
Each recipe makes 1 cocktail

Just as the name suggests, the Corpse Reviver No. 2 was a drink meant to bring you back to life. A hangover cure, if you will, often consumed in the morning after a night of imbibing. It is personally one of my absolute favorite gin cocktails, but I'm not sure if this drink would bring me back to life or just keep me feeling tipsy. The Corpse Reviver No. 2 belongs to a family of cocktails from the 1870s—though many of the other variations have been lost to time. As an "equal parts" cocktail, it is fun to play around with the recipe. Swap out the gin for tequila or pisco, the orange liqueur for passion fruit or melon. Choose your own "reviver" adventure, like I did with my modern twist, Back for More. Mezcal brings in a touch of smokiness and the blue Curaçao will have people turning heads.

CLASSIC CORPSE REVIVER NO. 2	RIFF BACK FOR MORE	N—A NINE LIVES
GLASSWARE coupe	**GLASSWARE** coupe	**GLASSWARE** highball
Absinthe (see Pro Tip), for rinsing ¾ ounce gin ¾ ounce Lillet Blanc ¾ ounce orange liqueur ¾ ounce fresh lemon juice Fresh cherry, for garnish	Absinthe (see Pro Tip), for rinsing ¾ ounce mezcal ¾ ounce Pinot Gris ¾ ounce blue Curaçao ¾ ounce Acidified Grapefruit Juice (page 34) 1 dash orange bitters Grapefruit twist, for garnish	1 ounce spirit-free gin ¾ ounce Martini & Rossi nonalcoholic Floreale aperitivo ½ ounce blanc verjus ½ ounce Lemon Oleo-Saccharum (page 31) 2 ounces tonic water Lemon twist, for garnish
Rinse the inside of a coupe glass with absinthe. ("Rinsing" a glass entails adding a small amount of spirit to an empty glass and swirling it around to coat the inside.) In a shaker tin, combine the gin, Lillet Blanc, orange liqueur, and lemon juice. Add cubed ice and shake vigorously for 12 seconds. Fine-strain into the prepared coupe. Garnish with a cherry.	Rinse the inside of a coupe glass with absinthe. Combine the mezcal, pinot gris, blue Curaçao, acidified grapefruit juice, and orange bitters. Add cubed ice and shake vigorously for 12 seconds. Fine-strain into the prepared coupe and garnish with a grapefruit twist.	In a shaker tin, combine the spirit-free gin, Floreale aperitivo, blanc verjus, and lemon oleo-saccharum. Add cubed ice and shake vigorously for 7 seconds. Fine-strain into a highball glass over fresh ice and top with tonic water. Gently stir to incorporate and garnish with a lemon twist.

 **PRO TIP** Fill an atomizer with absinthe and spritz the inside of your glass instead of rinsing it. This will ensure you get an even coat as well as leave you with less waste.

Left to right: Corpse Reviver No. 2, Nine Lives, Back for More

Left to right: Ru-Paulitan, Metropolitan, Cosmopolitan

COSMOPOLITAN

1985
Each recipe makes 1 cocktail

From the Rainbow Room to Madonna to *Sex and the City,* the Cosmopolitan has lived many lives. In the late '80s, vodka was king. Drinks like the Sea Breeze, Woo Woo, and Kamikaze were gaining more and more popularity. Enter bartender Toby Cecchini's Cosmopolitan. Essentially just a Kamikaze with cranberry juice added, this drink was on everyone's lips. Fast-forward to the '90s when the Cosmopolitan took center stage on the hit show *Sex and the City*. You couldn't go to a bar without seeing someone sipping on this pink drink. It's tart, slightly sweet, and oh so crushable. The Ru-Paulitan, my modern twist on the Cosmo, is a nod to one of my current favorite shows, *RuPaul's Drag Race*. Can I get an Amen?

CLASSIC COSMOPOLITAN	**RIFF** RU–PAULITAN	**N–A** METROPOLITAN
GLASSWARE martini	**GLASSWARE** Nick & Nora	**GLASSWARE** coupe
1½ ounces citron vodka ¾ ounce orange liqueur ¾ ounce unsweetened cranberry juice (see Pro Tip) ½ ounce fresh lime juice Orange peel, for garnish	1½ ounces vodka ¾ ounce limoncello ½ ounce Earl Grey Oleo-Saccharum (page 31) ¾ ounce Cranberry Shrub (page 33) ½ ounce fresh lemon juice Orange peel, for garnish	1½ ounces Seedlip Grove 42 nonalcoholic spirit ½ ounce Wilfred's nonalcoholic aperitif ½ ounce Grapefruit Oleo-Saccharum (page 31) 2 ounces white cranberry juice ½ ounce fresh lime juice Rosemary sprig, for garnish
In a shaker tin, combine the citron vodka, orange liqueur, cranberry juice, and lime juice. Add cubed ice and shake vigorously for 12 seconds. Fine-strain into a martini glass and garnish with an orange peel.	In a shaker tin, combine the vodka, limoncello, Earl Grey oleo-saccharum, cranberry shrub, and lemon juice. Add cubed ice and shake vigorously for 12 seconds. Fine-strain into a Nick & Nora glass and garnish with an orange peel.	In a shaker tin, combine the Seedlip Grove, nonalcoholic aperitif, grapefruit oleo-saccharum, white cranberry juice, and lime juice. Add cubed ice and shake vigorously for 10 seconds. Fine-strain into a coupe and garnish with a rosemary sprig.

PRO TIP By using unsweetened cranberry juice you have more control over the sweetness of your drink. If you plan on using sweetened cranberry juice, use less orange liqueur.

DAIQUIRI

1898
Each recipe makes 1 cocktail

The daiquiri, named after the town in Cuba it was invented in, is quite possibly the most famous three-ingredient drink, certainly the most famous rum drink. The daiquiri is the prime example that sometimes less is more. You would think this drink would be impossible to mess up, but the daiquiri relies heavily on balance. For many, the daiquiri is used as a "litmus" test to see if the bartender is capable of making a decent drink. Blended, shaken, flavored—I'll take a daiquiri any way I can get it. A fun way to put your own spin on a daiquiri is to use a blend of rums, like I did with the Daiquiri Inquiry. Each rum has its own unique flavor profile; by blending them together you get even more depth of flavor without adding in any more ingredients.

CLASSIC DAIQUIRI	RIFF DAIQUIRI INQUIRY	N—A DESTINATION DAIQUIRI
GLASSWARE coupe	**GLASSWARE** Nick & Nora	**GLASSWARE** rocks
2 ounces white rum ¾ ounce fresh lime juice ¾ ounce Simple Syrup (page 26) Lime wheel, for garnish	1 ounce white rum 1 ounce rhum agricole ¾ ounce fresh lime juice ½ ounce Demerara Syrup (page 25) 1 sprig rosemary 1 grapefruit peel 2 drops Saline Solution (page 40) Rosemary sprig and grapefruit twist, for garnish	1½ ounces Seedlip Grove 42 nonalcoholic spirit ½ fresh passion fruit seeds ½ ounce fresh lime juice ¾ ounce Simple Syrup (page 26) Passion fruit half and a mint sprig
In a shaker tin, combine the white rum, lime juice, and simple syrup. Add cubed ice and shake vigorously for 12 seconds. Strain into a coupe glass and garnish with a lime wheel.	In a shaker tin, combine the white rum, rhum agricole, lime juice, demerara syrup, rosemary sprig, grapefruit peel, and saline solution. Add cubed ice and shake vigorously for 12 seconds. Fine-strain into a Nick & Nora glass and garnish with a rosemary sprig and grapefruit twist.	In a shaker tin, combine the Seedlip Grove, passion fruit seeds, lime juice, and simple syrup. Add cubed ice and shake vigorously for 10 seconds. Fine-strain into a rocks glass over fresh ice. Garnish with half of a passion fruit and a mint sprig.

PRO TIP Shaking a cocktail with a piece of citrus peel is called a "regal shake." It adds a touch of bitterness and citrus oils without adding to the volume of the drink.

Left: Daiquiri Inquiry, *front:*
Destination Daiquiri, *back:* Daiquiri

EARL GREY MARTEANI

2000s

Each recipe makes 1 cocktail, except for the Lady Grey Milk Punch, which makes 4 cocktails

Tea is such an underutilized ingredient in cocktails. Not only does it add another layer of flavor, but it also adds tannins, which dry out your palette and draw you in for another sip. In this modern classic cocktail, innovative drink creator Audrey Saunders uses the notes of bergamot found in the Earl Grey tea to highlight the London dry gin. Just another easy way to elevate your classic cocktails. You can use tea to not only infuse a spirit but also as a lengthener in a punch style drink like I've done here with the Lady Grey Milk Punch, or use it as a replacement for a "base spirit" like in the Duke of Earl.

CLASSIC **EARL GREY MARTEANI**	RIFF **LADY GREY MILK PUNCH**	N—A **DUKE OF EARL**
GLASSWARE chilled coupe	**GLASSWARE** 4 chilled Nick & Noras	**GLASSWARE** rocks
1½ ounces Earl Grey Gin (page 37) ¾ ounce fresh lemon juice 1 ounce Simple Syrup (page 26) 1 egg white Lemon twist, for garnish	6 ounces gin 2 ounces Italicus bergamot liqueur 3 ounces fresh lemon juice 3 ounces Grapefruit Oleo-Saccharum (page 31) 4 ounces Brewed Earl Grey Tea (page 42) 4 ounces whole milk Grapefruit twist, for garnish	2 ounces Brewed Earl Grey Tea (page 42) ½ ounce Falernum (page 30) ½ ounce Grapefruit Oleo-Saccharum (page 31) 1 ounce Acidified Grapefruit Juice (page 34) Cinnamon stick, for garnish
In a shaker tin, combine the Earl Grey gin, lemon juice, simple syrup, and egg white. Dry shake (without ice) for 10 seconds. Open the shaker tin, add cubed ice, and shake again for another 12 seconds. Fine-strain into a chilled coupe glass. Garnish with a lemon twist.	In a large container, combine the gin, Italicus, lemon juice, grapefruit oleo-saccharum, and Earl Grey tea. In a medium saucepan, heat the milk over medium-low heat. Once the milk has come to a simmer, remove from the heat and combine with the punch mix. Do not stir. Place the punch mix, uncovered, in the fridge and let sit for 3 to 4 hours (or longer). The mix should naturally separate.	In a shaker tin, combine the Earl Grey tea, falernum, grapefruit oleo-saccharum, and acidified grapefruit juice. Add cubed ice and shake vigorously for 10 seconds. Fine-strain into a rocks glass and garnish with a cinnamon stick.

Once the punch mix has settled, carefully and slowly strain through a coffee filter or tight-weave cheesecloth into a clean container, until the mix is clear. To ensure a crystal-clear finish, do not rush the straining process (see Pro Tip). You may need to filter the mix two or three times. Bottle and refrigerate until ready to serve.

To serve, pour 4½ ounces of the punch mix into a chilled Nick & Nora glass and garnish with a grapefruit twist.

 PRO TIP When making a milk punch, be sure to let the solids (curds) settle in the coffee filter when straining. Try not to agitate the solids in the filter, so that the mixture can run through clear. The curds act as a secondary filter and help achieve that crystal-clear finish.

Left to right: Duke of Earl, Earl Grey Marteani, Lady Grey Milk Punch

Left to right: Devil in a Blueb–Dress,
El Diablo, Devils in the Details

EL DIABLO

1940s
Each recipe makes 1 cocktail

El Diablo seems to always take a back seat to its more popular tequila cocktail cousins, the Paloma or margarita. But it shouldn't! The El Diablo has plenty to offer. It first appeared in print in *Trader Vic's Book of Food & Drink,* which was published in 1946. The combination of cassis and ginger beer really highlights the aged tequila—it's refreshing and packs a sneaky punch. If ginger beer isn't your thing, try swapping it out with its milder counterpart, ginger ale. The modern twist and zero-proof recipes highlight the El Diablo's versatility by using blackberry and blueberry, both excellent when paired with tequila.

CLASSIC EL DIABLO	RIFF DEVILS IN THE DETAILS	N—A DEVIL IN A BLUEB-DRESS
GLASSWARE collins	**GLASSWARE** collins	**GLASSWARE** collins
1½ ounces reposado tequila ½ ounce crème de cassis ½ ounce fresh lime juice 3 ounces ginger beer Lime wheel, for garnish	1½ ounces Blackberry Tequila (page 37) ½ ounce Ancho Reyes chile liqueur ½ ounce Falernum (page 30) ½ ounce fresh lime juice 3 ounces ginger beer Grated cinnamon and blackberry, for garnish	1½ ounces spirit-free tequila 1 tablespoon blueberry jam ½ ounce fresh lime juice 2 dashes orange bitters 3 ounces ginger beer Blueberry, for garnish
In a shaker tin, combine the tequila, crème de cassis, and lime juice. Add cubed ice and shake vigorously for 7 seconds. Fine-strain into a collins glass over fresh ice and top with ginger beer. Gently stir to incorporate and garnish with a lime wheel.	In a shaker tin, combine the infused tequila, Ancho Reyes, falernum, and lime juice. Add cubed ice and shake vigorously for 7 seconds. Fine-strain into a collins glass over fresh ice and top off with ginger beer. Gently stir to incorporate and garnish with grated cinnamon and a blackberry.	In a shaker tin, combine the spirit-free tequila, blueberry jam, lime juice, and orange bitters. Add cubed ice and shake vigorously for 7 seconds. Fine-strain into a collins glass over fresh ice and top off with ginger beer. Gently stir to incorporate and garnish with a blueberry.

 PRO TIP Be careful not to overshake a drink that has a lengthener. The lengthener will also act as secondary dilution.

ENZONI

2002
Each recipe makes 1 cocktail

Created in the early 2000s by bartender Vincenzo Errico at Match Bar in London, this drink was ahead of its time. Bridging the gap between the Negroni and gin sour, the Enzoni is the best of both worlds—a great aperitif-style cocktail that satisfies those bitter taste buds as well as a crushable sour for the ones who like their drinks a bit more on the tart side. Switch up the grape varietal and you'll see just how much this cocktail changes. If you've never tried a Cotton Candy grape before, make a note of when they are in season and make sure to try them in the modern twist, Friendzoni.

CLASSIC ENZONI	RIFF FRIENDZONI	N—A COUSIN VINNY
GLASSWARE rocks	**GLASSWARE** rocks	**GLASSWARE** rocks
5 seedless green grapes 1 ounce gin 1 ounce Campari ¾ ounce fresh lemon juice ½ ounce Simple Syrup (page 26) Green grape, for garnish	5 Cotton Candy grapes (see Pro Tip) 1 ounce gin 1 ounce Aperol ¾ ounce fresh lemon juice ½ ounce Simple Syrup (page 26) Cotton Candy grape, for garnish	5 seedless red grapes 1 ounce spirit-free gin ¾ ounce Ghia nonalcoholic aperitif ¾ ounce blanc verjus ½ ounce Rich Simple Syrup (page 26) Red grape, for garnish
In a shaker tin, combine the grapes, gin, Campari, lemon juice, and simple syrup. Gently muddle the grapes, just enough to break them up. Add cubed ice and shake vigorously for 12 seconds. Fine-strain into a rocks glass over fresh ice. Garnish with a green grape.	In a shaker tin, combine the grapes, gin, Aperol, lemon juice, and simple syrup. Gently muddle the grapes, just enough to break them up. Add cubed ice and shake vigorously for 12 seconds. Fine-strain into a rocks glass over fresh ice. Garnish with a Cotton Candy grape.	In a shaker tin, combine the grapes, spirit-free gin, Ghia, blanc verjus, and rich simple syrup. Gently muddle the grapes, just enough to break them up. Add cubed ice and shake vigorously for 10 seconds. Fine-strain into a rocks glass over fresh ice. Garnish with a red grape.

PRO TIP Cotton Candy grapes aren't always readily available. I suggest storing a batch in your freezer so you can enjoy them all year long. Frozen grapes will generally last up to a year in the freezer, just be sure to remove them from the vine first.

Enzoni

Left to right: Espresso Martini, Death Before Decaf, Bean Around the World

ESPRESSO MARTINI

1980s
Each recipe makes 1 cocktail

We have bartending legend Dick Bradsell and a famous model to thank for the creation of the Espresso Martini. Legend has it that a certain "top model" walked into the Soho Brasserie in London and asked Dick to make her something that was going to "Wake me up and f*ck me up!" And so, the Espresso Martini was born. Although the original recipe is really quite simple, there are so many ways to make this classic drink your own. For my modern twist and zero-proof recipe, I wanted to highlight how versatile coffee in cocktails can be, especially when pairing it with a touch of spice or using tonic water to make it a long refreshing drink.

`CLASSIC` ESPRESSO MARTINI	`RIFF` BEAN AROUND THE WORLD	`N—A` DEATH BEFORE DECAF
GLASSWARE chilled martini	**GLASSWARE** chilled coupe	**GLASSWARE** collins
2 ounces vodka ½ ounce coffee liqueur 1 ounce espresso ½ ounce Simple Syrup (page 26) 3 coffee beans, for garnish	1½ ounces reposado tequila ¾ ounce coffee liqueur ½ ounce Ancho Reyes chile liqueur 1 ounce Cold Brew Coffee (page 39) ½ ounce Simple Syrup (page 26) 1 dash chocolate bitters Lemon twist and 3 coffee beans, for garnish	½ ounce Lemon Oleo-Saccharum (page 31) 1 dash orange bitters 4 ounces tonic water 2 ounces espresso, at room temperature (see Pro Tip) Lemon coin, for garnish
In a shaker tin, combine the vodka, coffee liqueur, espresso, and simple syrup. Add cubed ice and shake vigorously for 12 seconds. Fine-strain into a chilled martini glass and garnish with the coffee beans.	In a shaker tin, combine the tequila, coffee liqueur, chile liqueur, coffee, simple syrup, and bitters. Add cubed ice and shake vigorously for 12 seconds. Fine-strain into a chilled coupe glass and garnish with a lemon twist and coffee beans.	In a collins glass, combine the lemon oleo-saccharum and orange bitters. Fill the glass with ice cubes and add the tonic water. Gently stir to incorporate, being careful not to agitate the bubbles too much. Slowly add the espresso on top to give a layered effect. Garnish with a lemon coin.

PRO TIP Let your espresso come down to room temperature before adding to your cocktail shaker. You don't want the hot espresso to melt your ice, causing your drink to be overdiluted.

FISH HOUSE PUNCH

1794
Each recipe makes 8 to 10 cocktails

The first written reference to the Fish House Punch was in 1794 and it is the most famous punch of them all. Originating in Philadelphia at a fishing and social club, this drink is best enjoyed the traditional way—in a large punch bowl served over a big ol' block of ice, in the company of your mates. There are no real rules when it comes to punches, although using an oleo-saccharum as a base to maximize flavor is always encouraged. Follow the classic recipe or try something a little outside the box.

CLASSIC FISH HOUSE PUNCH	RIFF HOUSE PARTY PUNCH	N—A TOTAL KNOCKOUT
GLASSWARE punch bowl and cups	**GLASSWARE** punch bowl and cups	**GLASSWARE** punch bowls and cups
750ml Jamaican rum 12 ounces Cognac 12 ounces peach brandy or peach liqueur 12 cups cold water 2 cups fresh lemon juice 2 cups Lemon Oleo-Saccharum (page 31) Grated nutmeg, for garnish	750ml pisco 12 ounces fino sherry 12 ounces passion fruit liqueur 12 cups strongly Brewed Chamomile Tea (page 41) 2 cups fresh lemon juice 2 cups Grapefruit Oleo-Saccharum (page 31) 4 cups whole milk Chamomile flowers, for garnish	12 cups strongly Brewed Black Tea (page 42) 3 cups peach puree 3 cups fresh lemon juice 2 cups Orange Oleo-Saccharum (page 31) 4 cinnamon sticks 2 cups whole milk Grated cinnamon, for garnish
In a large punch bowl, combine the rum, Cognac, peach brandy, water, lemon juice, and lemon oleo-saccharum. Mix thoroughly. Carefully add a large solid block of ice to the punch bowl. Generously grate nutmeg over the top and serve.	In a large container, combine the pisco, sherry, passion fruit liqueur, tea, lemon juice, and grapefruit oleo-saccharum. In a medium saucepan, heat the milk over medium-low heat. Once the milk has come to a simmer, remove from the heat and combine with the punch base. Do not stir. Place the punch mix, uncovered, in the fridge and let sit for 3 to 4 hours (or longer). The mix should naturally separate.	In a large container, combine the tea, peach puree, lemon juice, orange oleo-saccharum, and cinnamon sticks. In a small saucepan, heat the milk over medium-low heat. Once it has come to a simmer, remove from the heat and combine with the punch base. Do not stir. Place the punch mix in the fridge, uncovered, and let sit for 3 to 4 hours (or longer). The mix should naturally separate.

HOUSE PARTY PUNCH, continued

Once the punch mix has settled, carefully and slowly strain through a coffee filter or tight-weave cheesecloth into a clean container until the mix is clear. To ensure a crystal-clear finish, do not rush the straining process. You may need to filter the mix two or three times.

Bottle and refrigerate the punch until you are ready to serve. Pour the punch mix into an ice-filled glass and garnish with chamomile flowers.

TOTAL KNOCKOUT, continued

Once the punch mix has settled, carefully and slowly strain the entire mix through a coffee filter or tight-weave cheesecloth into a clean container until the mix is clear. To ensure a crystal-clear finish, do not rush the straining process. You may need to filter the mix two or three times.

Bottle and refrigerate the punch until you are ready to serve.

 PRO TIP When making your oleo-saccharum, try to remove as much of the pith as possible from your citrus peels. Too much pith and your oleo will have a bitter aftertaste.

Left to right: Front Tuck, Flip, Somersault

FLIP

1600s
Each recipe makes 1 cocktail

First appearing in print in the late 1600s in a play written by William Congreve, *Love for Love,* the flip is definitely more obscure than most cocktails. It was originally made from a combination of ale, brandy, and sugar and heated with a hot poker. It wasn't until the flip made its way to America that the ale was replaced with a whole egg and served cold. The thought of drinking a whole egg might scare some people off, but if you have ever liked sipping eggnog or have enjoyed crème anglaise, you have nothing to worry about. The flip is a rich, dessert-like cocktail full of history and, well, protein.

CLASSIC FLIP	RIFF FRONT TUCK	N—A SOMERSAULT
GLASSWARE chilled coupe	**GLASSWARE** chilled Nick & Nora	**GLASSWARE** rocks
2 ounces oloroso sherry ½ ounce Simple Syrup (page 26) 1 egg Grated nutmeg, for garnish	1 ounce Amontillado sherry 1 ounce amaretto ½ ounce maple syrup 1 egg Grated nutmeg, for garnish	1½ ounces Seedlip Spice 94 nonalcoholic spirit ¾ ounce Cold Brew Coffee (page 39) ¾ ounce maple syrup 1 ounce heavy cream 1 egg Coffee beans, for garnish
In a shaker tin, combine the oloroso sherry, simple syrup, and egg. Dry shake (without ice) for 10 seconds. Open the shaker tin, add cubed ice, and shake again for another 12 seconds. Fine-strain into a chilled coupe. Garnish with grated nutmeg.	In a shaker tin, combine the Amontillado sherry, amaretto, maple syrup, and egg. Dry shake (without ice) for 10 seconds. Open the shaker tin, add cubed ice, and shake again for another 12 seconds. Fine-strain into a chilled Nick & Nora glass. Garnish with grated nutmeg.	In a shaker tin, combine the Seedlip Spice, cold brew coffee, maple syrup, heavy cream, and egg. Dry shake (without ice) for 10 seconds. Open the shaker tin, add cubed ice, and shake again for another 12 seconds. Fine-strain into a rocks glass over one large cube of ice. Garnish with coffee beans.

PRO TIP If you are squeamish about using raw eggs in cocktails, there are many plant-based alternatives you can use, such as aquafaba and vegan foamers.

FRENCH 75

1920s
Each recipe makes 1 cocktail

Named after the French 75-millimeter field gun, I promise you this drink is much friendlier than the name suggests. It is very likely that the first French 75s were made with Cognac rather than gin, but the history of this cocktail, like many classic cocktails, is a bit of a mystery. What I do know is that it makes for an excellent brunch drink. The modern twist, Eiffel 65, adds a touch of orange liqueur as a nod to another great brunch drink, the mimosa. If gin isn't your thing, feel free to use any spirit of your choice. Vodka, tequila, or pisco will work—or give the Cognac version a try. And of course, there's always the zero-proof option.

CLASSIC FRENCH 75	RIFF EIFFEL 65	N—A THE 1975
GLASSWARE flute	GLASSWARE coupe	GLASSWARE flute
1 ounce gin ½ fresh lemon juice ½ ounce Simple Syrup (page 26) 1 dash orange bitters 3 ounces Champagne Lemon twist, for garnish	1 ounce gin ½ ounce blue Curaçao ½ ounce Lemon Oleo-Saccharum (page 31) ½ ounce fresh lemon juice 1 dash orange bitters 2 ounces Champagne Orange twist, for garnish	1 ounce spirit-free gin ½ ounce Acidified Grapefruit Juice (page 34) ½ ounce Lemon Oleo-Saccharum (page 31) 1 dash orange bitters 3 ounces nonalcoholic sparkling wine Grapefruit twist, for garnish
In a shaker tin, combine the gin, lemon juice, simple syrup, and orange bitters. Add cubed ice and shake vigorously for 10 seconds. Fine-strain into a flute and top with Champagne. Garnish with a lemon twist.	In a shaker tin, combine the gin, blue Curaçao, lemon oleo-saccharum, lemon juice, and orange bitters. Add cubed ice and shake vigorously for 10 seconds. Fine-strain into a coupe and top with Champagne. Garnish with an orange twist.	In a shaker tin, combine the spirit-free gin, acidified grapefruit juice, lemon oleo-saccharum, and orange bitters. Add cubed ice and shake vigorously for 10 seconds. Fine-strain into a flute and garnish with a grapefruit twist.

PRO TIP Tilt your flute to the side when pouring in your Champagne. This will help keep the bubbles from overflowing your glass.

Left to right: The 1975,
Eiffel 65, French 75

Left to right: Garibaldi, Claribaldi

GARIBALDI

2015
Each recipe makes 1 cocktail

Although the Garibaldi has been around for a lot longer than 2015, it was a relatively obscure cocktail until bartender Naren Young of New York City's Dante put it on their menu. Named after Giuseppe Garibaldi, an integral figure in the liberation of both Italy and Uruguay, it's a simple combination of orange juice and Campari. But what makes this cocktail so special is how the orange juice is prepared. It has to be freshly squeezed and it has to be blended so it's "fluffy." Blending introduces air as well as texture into the drink. But if "fluffy" isn't your thing, try your hand at the Claribaldi. In this version, the orange juice is treated with clarifying agents typically used in wine making for a crystal-clear interpretation of this iconic drink.

CLASSIC **GARIBALDI**	RIFF **CLARIBALDI**	N—A **BITTER BANGER**
GLASSWARE juice glass	**GLASSWARE** juice glass	**GLASSWARE** rocks
4 ounces freshly squeezed orange juice 1½ ounces Campari Bar spoon of Rich Simple Syrup (page 26) Orange wedge, for garnish	1 ounce Campari ½ ounce Milk Liqueur (page 39) 4 ounces Clarified Orange Juice (page 39) 1 dash Acid Blend (page 34) Orange coin, for garnish	1 ounce Ghia nonalcoholic aperitif ½ ounce Vanilla Bean Syrup (page 27) 2 ounces Acidified Orange Juice (page 34) Orange twist, for garnish
Fine-strain the orange juice to remove any pulp. Then blend the juice on high in a blender, without ice, to make it "fluffy." Pour the Campari and rich simple syrup into a juice glass with 2 or 3 cubes of ice and stir. Add another 2 or 3 cubes of ice and fill the remainder of the glass with the fluffy orange juice. Garnish with an orange wedge.	In a shaker tin, combine the Campari, milk liqueur, clarified orange juice, and acid blend. Add cubed ice and "throw" the mix back and forth between the two parts of the shaker tin, 8 to 10 times. Strain into a juice glass over fresh ice and garnish with an orange coin.	In a shaker tin, combine the Ghia, vanilla syrup, and acidified orange juice. Add cubed ice and shake vigorously for 12 seconds. Fine-strain into a rocks glass over fresh ice and garnish with an orange twist.

PRO TIP If you can't have orange juice or just want something different, try these drinks with fluffy pineapple or watermelon juice.

GIN BASIL SMASH

2008
Each recipe makes 1 cocktail

Created by bartender Joerg Meyer in Hamburg, Germany, this drink was originally called the Gin Pesto. But as the drink grew in popularity, the name changed to describe its preparation. The "smash" is a style of cocktail, similar to a julep, which refers to the ice smashing against the basil or mint inside the cocktail shaker, breaking up the leaves. Being that this drink is more about the style of preparation, you can make a smash with just about any fresh fruit and herbs. The combination of basil and mint makes for a fresh, herbaceous Garden Smash, whereas watermelon with basil makes you feel like you're on summer vacation.

CLASSIC GIN BASIL SMASH	RIFF GARDEN SMASH	N–A SUMMER SMASH
GLASSWARE rocks	**GLASSWARE** rocks	**GLASSWARE** rocks
2 ounces gin ¾ ounce fresh lemon juice ¾ ounce Simple Syrup (page 26) 3 or 4 fresh basil leaves Fresh basil leaf, for garnish	1½ ounces gin ¼ ounce Liquore Strega ¾ ounce fresh lemon juice ½ ounce Simple Syrup (page 26) 2 drops Saline Solution (page 40) 3 or 4 fresh basil leaves 3 or 4 fresh mint leaves Fresh basil and mint leaves, for garnish	1 ounce spirit-free gin ½ ounce yuzu juice ½ ounce Rich Simple Syrup (page 26) 3 cubes of watermelon 4 fresh basil leaves Watermelon triangle and basil leaves, for garnish
In a shaker tin, combine the gin, lemon juice, simple syrup, and basil leaves. Add cubed ice and shake vigorously for 12 seconds. Fine-strain into a rocks glass over fresh ice and garnish with a fresh basil leaf.	In a shaker tin, combine the gin, Strega, lemon juice, simple syrup, saline solution, basil, and mint leaves. Add cubed ice and shake vigorously for 12 seconds. Fine-strain into a rocks glass over fresh ice and garnish with fresh basil and mint leaves.	In a shaker tin, combine the spirit-free gin, yuzu juice, rich simple syrup, watermelon cubes, and basil leaves. Gently muddle. Add cubed ice and shake vigorously for 12 seconds. Fine-strain into a rocks glass over fresh ice and garnish with a watermelon triangle and fresh basil leaves.

 PRO TIP By themselves, softer herbs like mint and basil don't need muddling. When shaking, the ice will break up their leaves without making them overly bitter.

Summer Smash

Left: **24K Gold**, *bottom right:* **Gold Rush**, *top right:* **Golden Nugget**

GOLD RUSH

2001
Each recipe makes 1 cocktail

Here's another simple three-ingredient drink that packs a ton of flavor. Similar to a whiskey sour or Bee's Knees, the Gold Rush utilizes honey as both a sweetener and flavor enhancer. It was made famous at the iconic Milk & Honey bar in New York City by longtime friends and legendary bartenders T. J. Siegal and Sasha Petraske. With so many varieties of honey to choose from, whether it is sourced locally or from somewhere far-off and exotic, the one you choose will certainly impact the flavor of your drink. Experiment with making your own flavored honey syrups, like the ginger honey used in the Golden Nugget.

`CLASSIC` GOLD RUSH	`RIFF` GOLDEN NUGGET	`N—A` 24K GOLD
GLASSWARE rocks	**GLASSWARE** rocks	**GLASSWARE** chilled Nick & Nora
2 ounces bourbon ¾ ounce fresh lemon juice ¾ ounce Honey Syrup (page 28) Lemon twist, for garnish	2 ounces rye whiskey ¼ ounce Fireball Cinnamon Whisky ¾ ounce Acidified Grapefruit Juice (page 34) ¾ ounce Ginger Honey Syrup (page 28) Grapefruit twist and grated cinnamon, for garnish	2 ounces carrot juice ¾ ounce fresh lemon juice ¾ ounce Ginger Honey Syrup (page 28) 2 dashes aromatic bitters 3 drops olive oil and candied ginger, for garnish
In a shaker tin, combine the bourbon, lemon juice, and honey syrup. Add cubed ice and shake vigorously for 12 seconds. Fine-strain into a rocks glass over fresh ice and garnish with a lemon twist.	In a shaker tin, combine the rye, Fireball, acidified grapefruit juice, and ginger honey syrup. Add cubed ice and shake vigorously for 12 seconds. Fine-strain into a rocks glass over fresh ice and garnish with a grapefruit twist and grated cinnamon.	In a shaker tin, combine the carrot juice, lemon juice, ginger honey syrup, and aromatic bitters. Add cubed ice and shake vigorously for 12 seconds. Fine-strain into a chilled Nick & Nora glass. Garnish with olive oil and candied ginger.

PRO TIP Make sure to store your honey syrups in the fridge. Once water is introduced, the syrup will start to ferment into mead if left out at room temperature.

GRASSHOPPER

1919
Each recipe makes 1 cocktail

New Orleans is the birthplace of so many delicious classic cocktails, and the Grasshopper is one of them. Originally created at Tujague's by owner Phillip Guichet in 1919, this green cocktail tastes like a delicious glass of melted mint chocolate chip ice cream. I would most definitely classify this as a dessert cocktail. In my version, I like to break up the richness with the addition of gin and a touch of green Chartreuse.

CLASSIC **GRASSHOPPER**	RIFF **MR. MIYAGI**	N—A **GREEN BELT**
GLASSWARE chilled coupe	**GLASSWARE** chilled Nick & Nora	**GLASSWARE** chilled rocks
1 ounce green crème de menthe 1 ounce white crème de cacao 1 ounce heavy cream Grated nutmeg, for garnish	1 ounce gin ½ ounce Giffard Menthe-Pastille ½ ounce white crème de cacao ¼ ounce green Chartreuse 2 ounces heavy cream Dark chocolate shavings, for garnish	1 ounce spirit-free gin 2 ounces coconut milk 1 scoop mint chocolate chip ice cream 3 fresh mint leaves Mint sprig, for garnish
In a shaker tin, combine the crème de menthe, crème de cacao, and heavy cream. Add cubed ice and shake vigorously for 12 seconds. Fine-strain into a chilled coupe glass and garnish with grated nutmeg.	In a shaker tin, combine the gin, menthe-pastille, crème de cacao, green Chartreuse, and heavy cream. Add cubed ice and shake vigorously for 12 seconds. Fine-strain into a chilled Nick & Nora glass. Garnish with dark chocolate shavings.	In a blender, combine the spirit-free gin, coconut milk, mint chocolate chip ice cream, and mint leaves and blend on high until smooth. Pour into a chilled rocks glass and garnish with a sprig of mint.

PRO TIP Place your serving glass in the freezer a few minutes prior to making your drink. This will help keep your drink nice and cold from start to finish.

Green Belt

Left to right: Six-Toed Cat, Room 511, Hemingway Daiquiri

HEMINGWAY DAIQUIRI

1930s
Each recipe makes 1 cocktail

Don't be fooled. Although it bears his name, Hemingway was not the creator of this drink, but rather the inspiration for it. He spent many years in Havana but preferred his daiquiris with double the rum and no sugar, often referred to as a Papa Doble. But just because Hemingway enjoyed them that way doesn't mean they were any good, so the recipe was tweaked to be more palatable and balanced with the addition of Maraschino liqueur to bring in that much-needed sweetness. To continue to pay homage to Hemingway, the Six-Toed Cat and Room 511 are named after Hemingway's love for polydactyl cats and the hotel room he stayed in for almost a decade in Cuba. Room 511 has since been preserved as a tiny monument to the Nobel Prize–winning author.

CLASSIC HEMINGWAY DAIQUIRI	RIFF SIX-TOED CAT	N-A ROOM 511
GLASSWARE chilled coupe	**GLASSWARE** collins	**GLASSWARE** rocks
2 ounces white rum ½ ounce Maraschino liqueur ¾ ounce fresh lime juice ½ ounce grapefruit juice Lime wheel, for garnish	1 ounce white rum 1 ounce cachaça ¼ ounce crème de violette liqueur ½ ounce fresh lime juice ½ ounce Demerara Syrup (page 25) 1 grapefruit peel 3 ounces grapefruit soda Grapefruit twist, for garnish	2 ounces Brewed Lavender Tea (page 41) 1 ounce fresh grapefruit juice ½ ounce fresh lemon juice ½ ounce Orgeat (page 30) Dried lavender sprig, for garnish
In a shaker tin, combine the white rum, Maraschino liqueur, lime juice, and grapefruit juice. Add cubed ice and shake vigorously for 12 seconds. Fine-strain into a chilled coupe glass and garnish with a lime wheel.	In a shaker tin, combine the white rum, cachaça, crème de violette, lime juice, demerara syrup, and grapefruit peel. Add cubed ice and shake vigorously for 10 seconds. Fine-strain into a collins glass over fresh ice and top with grapefruit soda. Gently stir to incorporate and garnish with a grapefruit twist.	In a shaker tin, combine the lavender tea, grapefruit juice, lemon juice, and orgeat. Add cubed ice and shake vigorously for 10 seconds. Fine-strain into a rocks glass over fresh ice and garnish with a lavender sprig.

 PRO TIP If you need a substitute for Maraschino liqueur, try using kirsch or cherry heering. Just make sure to taste and adjust for balance as needed.

HOTEL GEORGIA

1940s
Each recipe makes 1 cocktail

Named after the historic hotel in downtown Vancouver, the Hotel Georgia is a gin sour with a subtle floral finish. Using orgeat as a sweetener brings in a nice nutty, almond flavor that is even further enhanced by the orange blossom water. The Hotel Georgia was built in 1927, but the cocktail wasn't established until the 1940s and didn't appear in print until 1951 in Ted Saucier's book *Bottoms Up*. The Hotel Georgia, now the Rosewood Hotel Georgia, still stands today at the corner of Georgia and Howe Streets. Each variation of this cocktail aims to enhance the floral and nutty nuances of the original cocktail. As a Vancouverite myself, it is always a pleasure to introduce this cocktail to those who have yet to try it.

CLASSIC HOTEL GEORGIA	RIFF ROOM WITH A VIEW	N—A THE NOMAD
GLASSWARE chilled coupe	**GLASSWARE** chilled coupe	**GLASSWARE** chilled coupe
2 ounces gin ½ ounce Orgeat (page 30) ¾ ounce fresh lemon juice 6 drops orange blossom water 1 egg white Lemon twist, for garnish	1½ ounces gin ½ ounce manzanilla sherry ½ ounce Orgeat (page 30) ¾ ounce Acidified Orange Juice (page 34) 1 dash orange bitters 1 egg white Grated nutmeg, for garnish	2 ounces spirit-free gin ¾ ounce Orgeat (page 30) ¾ ounce Acidified Grapefruit Juice (page 34) 3 drops rose water 1 egg white Grapefruit twist, for garnish
In a shaker tin, combine the gin, orgeat, lemon juice, orange blossom water, and egg white. Dry shake (without ice) for 10 seconds. Open the shaker tin, add cubed ice, and shake again for another 12 seconds. Fine-strain into a chilled coupe and garnish with a lemon twist.	In a shaker tin, combine the gin, manzanilla sherry, orgeat, acidified orange juice, orange bitters, and egg white. Dry shake (without ice) for 10 seconds. Open the shaker tin, add cubed ice, and shake again for another 12 seconds. Fine-strain into a chilled coupe and garnish with grated nutmeg.	In a shaker tin, combine the spirit-free gin, orgeat, acidified grapefruit juice, rose water, and egg white. Dry shake (without ice) for 10 seconds. Open the shaker tin, add cubed ice, and shake again for another 12 seconds. Fine-strain into a chilled coupe and garnish with a grapefruit twist.

PRO TIP Orange blossom water is quite powerful—a little goes a long way. You can generally find it in the baking section of your grocery store or in the international aisle. Note that orange blossom water and orange bitters are not interchangeable.

Left to right: The Nomad, Room with a View, Hotel Georgia

Who's the Boss

HUGO SPRITZ

2000s
Each recipe makes 1 cocktail

The Hugo Spritz is the perfect alternative to its bitter counterparts, the Aperol spritz and the Campari spritz. Originating from the South Tyrol province in northern Italy, it is typically made with locally foraged elderflower syrup, which gives this drink its distinctive floral taste. Because this is such a simple serve, it is fun to play around with it. Try adding in a lychee to complement the elderflower or a slice of watermelon to make it a little more juicy.

`CLASSIC` HUGO SPRITZ	`RIFF` WATERMELON HUGO SPRITZ	`N—A` WHO'S THE BOSS
GLASSWARE wine	**GLASSWARE** collins	**GLASSWARE** wine
½ ounce elderflower liqueur 4 ounces sparkling wine 2 ounces soda water 2 sprigs mint Lime wheel, for garnish	1 ounce elderflower liqueur ½ ounce fino sherry ½ ounce fresh lime juice 2 chunks of watermelon 2 sprigs mint 4 ounces sparkling wine Watermelon wedge and mint sprig, for garnish	½ ounce elderflower syrup 1 ounce lychee juice ½ ounce fresh lemon juice 2 sprigs mint 3 ounces nonalcoholic sparkling wine Lychee and mint sprig, for garnish
In an ice-filled wine glass, combine the elderflower liqueur, sparkling wine, soda water, and mint sprigs. Gently stir to incorporate and garnish with a lime wheel.	In a shaker tin, combine the elderflower liqueur, fino sherry, lime juice, watermelon, and mint sprigs. Gently muddle to break up the watermelon. Add cubed ice and shake vigorously for 7 seconds. Fine-strain into a collins glass over fresh ice and top with sparkling wine. Gently stir to incorporate and garnish with a watermelon wedge and mint sprig.	In an ice-filled wine glass, combine the elderflower syrup, lychee juice, lemon juice, mint sprigs, and nonalcoholic sparkling wine. Gently stir to incorporate and garnish with a lychee and mint sprig.

PRO TIP Elderflower liqueur has a tendency to oxidize once opened, so don't be alarmed if your bottle turns a shade or two darker. Keep out of direct sunlight or store in the fridge.

JUNGLE BIRD

1970s
Each recipe makes 1 cocktail

Created by beverage director Jeffery Ong See Teik for the opening of the Kuala Lumpur Hilton in Malaysia, this tasty tropical drink combines the richness of dark rum, the bitterness of an Italian aperitif, and the brightness of freshly pressed pineapple juice. Unlike most tiki-style drinks, the Jungle Bird leans a little more toward the bitter side. It is the perfect combination of bitter, sweet, and sour. For the variations, I didn't want to stray too far away from the original concept, but rather show you how versatile the drink can be just by changing the base spirit.

CLASSIC JUNGLE BIRD	**RIFF** CITY PIGEON	**N–A** FREE BIRD
GLASSWARE collins	**GLASSWARE** collins	**GLASSWARE** collins
1½ ounces blackstrap rum ¾ ounce Campari 1½ ounces fresh pineapple juice (see Pro Tip) ½ ounce fresh lime juice ½ ounce Rich Simple Syrup (page 26) Pineapple wedge and pineapple leaves, for garnish	¾ ounce gin ¾ ounce blanco tequila ½ ounce Campari 1½ ounces fresh pineapple juice (see Pro Tip) ½ ounce fresh lime juice ½ ounce Rosemary Syrup (page 27) Rosemary sprig and lime wheel, for garnish	1½ ounces spirit-free gin 1½ ounces fresh pineapple juice (see Pro Tip) ½ ounce fresh lime juice ½ ounce Rich Simple Syrup (page 26) 1½ ounces Stappi Red Bitter soda Orange coin, for garnish
In a shaker tin, combine the rum, Campari, pineapple juice, lime juice, and rich simple syrup. Add cubed ice and shake vigorously for 12 seconds. Fine-strain into a collins glass over fresh ice. Garnish with a pineapple wedge and leaves.	In a shaker tin, combine the gin, tequila, Campari, pineapple juice, lime juice, and rosemary syrup. Add cubed ice and shake vigorously for 12 seconds. Fine-strain into a collins glass over fresh ice. Using a kitchen torch with extreme caution, lightly flame a rosemary sprig to release the aromatic oils and use as a garnish along with a lime wheel.	In a shaker tin, combine the spirit-free gin, pineapple juice, lime juice, and rich simple syrup. Add cubed ice and shake vigorously for 7 seconds. Fine-strain into a collins glass over fresh ice and top with Stappi Red Bitter soda. Garnish with the orange coin.

 PRO TIP Use an electric juicer to make freshly squeezed pineapple juice for a nice frothy finish to this drink.

Left to right: City Pigeon,
Jungle Bird, Free Bird

Left to right: Vancouver Buck, Kentucky Buck, Big Bucks

KENTUCKY BUCK

2008
Each recipe makes 1 cocktail

The "buck" is from a family of cocktails better known as the Horse's Neck. Once just a tall glass of nonalcoholic ginger ale, a shot of bourbon or brandy was added to give it an extra kick or "buck." Now, a buck is considered to be any spirit mixed with citrus and ginger ale or ginger beer. Erick Castro, the creator of the Kentucky Buck, adds seasonal strawberries and a dash of Angostura bitters to his variation for an extremely refreshing sip, which inspired my blueberry and blackberry variations.

CLASSIC KENTUCKY BUCK

GLASSWARE collins

2 ounces bourbon

¾ ounce fresh lemon juice

½ ounce Simple Syrup (page 26)

2 fresh strawberries, hulled

2 dashes Angostura bitters

3 ounces ginger beer

Lemon wheel and strawberry slice, for garnish

In a shaker tin, combine the bourbon, lemon juice, simple syrup, strawberries, and Angostura bitters. Gently muddle the strawberries, just enough to break them up. Add cubed ice and shake vigorously for 10 seconds. Fine-strain into a collins glass over fresh ice and top with ginger beer. Gently stir to incorporate and garnish with a lemon wheel and strawberry slice.

RIFF VANCOUVER BUCK

GLASSWARE collins

1½ ounces rye whiskey

½ ounce Blueberry Orange Liqueur (page 37)

½ ounce Rosemary Syrup (page 27)

¾ ounce fresh lime juice

8 fresh blueberries

1 dash orange bitters

3 ounces ginger beer

Lime wheel and fresh blueberries, for garnish

In a shaker tin, combine the rye, blueberry orange liqueur, rosemary syrup, lime juice, blueberries, and orange bitters. Gently muddle the blueberries, just enough to break them up. Add cubed ice and shake vigorously for 10 seconds. Fine-strain into a collins glass over fresh ice and top with ginger beer. Gently stir to incorporate and garnish with a lime wheel and several blueberries.

N-A BIG BUCKS

GLASSWARE collins

½ ounce Rosemary Syrup (page 27)

½ ounce fresh lime juice

2-inch piece peeled fresh ginger

3 fresh blackberries

1 dash nonalcoholic orange bitters

3 ounces ginger beer

Fresh blackberry, for garnish

In a shaker tin, combine the rosemary syrup, lime juice, ginger, blackberries, and orange bitters. Gently muddle the blackberries and ginger, just enough to break them up. Add cubed ice and shake vigorously for 10 seconds. Fine-strain into a collins glass over fresh ice and top with ginger beer. Gently stir to incorporate and garnish with a blackberry.

 PRO TIP To make these drinks even more refreshing, you can use homemade ginger syrup and soda water to replace the ginger beer.

KNICKERBOCKER

1862
Each recipe makes 1 cocktail

"Knickerbocker" was a term for a Dutch settler in New York, coined after the style of short pants they wore. A recipe for the Knickerbocker was first seen in print in 1862. The history of who or where it was first made is a bit of a mystery, but it was likely somewhere in New York. The drink relies heavily on the ingredients you use. For example, a quality raspberry syrup will make all the difference. The Knickerbocker is fresh and fruity and best enjoyed over shaved ice.

CLASSIC KNICKERBOCKER	RIFF DUTCH BOY	N—A NEW YORKER
GLASSWARE rocks	**GLASSWARE** coupe	**GLASSWARE** collins
2 ounces gold rum ½ ounce orange liqueur 1 ounce fresh lime juice ½ ounce Raspberry Syrup (page 27) Lime wheel and fresh raspberry, for garnish	1 ounce rhum agricole 1 ounce Raspberry Cognac (page 38) ½ ounce orange liqueur ¾ ounce fresh lime juice 3 fresh raspberries ½ ounce Simple Syrup (page 26) Fresh raspberry, for garnish	2 ounces Brewed Chamomile Tea (page 41) 1 ounce Acidified Raspberry Juice (page 34) ½ ounce Rich Simple Syrup (page 26) 1 orange wedge 2 ounces soda water Orange twist and fresh raspberry, for garnish
In a shaker tin, combine the gold rum, orange liqueur, lime juice, and raspberry syrup. Add cubed ice and shake vigorously for 12 seconds. Fine-strain into a rocks glass over pebble ice and garnish with a lime wheel and raspberry.	In a shaker tin, combine the rhum agricole, raspberry Cognac, orange liqueur, lime juice, raspberries, and simple syrup. Gently muddle the raspberries, just to break them up. Add cubed ice and shake vigorously for 12 seconds. Fine-strain into a coupe over one large piece of ice and garnish with a raspberry.	In a shaker tin, combine the chamomile tea, acidified raspberry juice, rich simple syrup, and orange wedge. Gently muddle the orange, just to break it up. Add cubed ice and shake vigorously for 10 seconds. Fine-strain into a collins glass over fresh ice and top with soda water. Gently stir to incorporate and garnish with an orange twist and raspberry.

PRO TIP If you don't have raspberry syrup available to you, simply muddle fresh raspberries and add ½ ounce of simple syrup.

Left to right: Dutch Boy,
New Yorker, Knickerbocker

Left to right: Lemon Drop Martini,
Sky-High Lemon Pie, Life's Lemons

LEMON DROP MARTINI

1970s
Each recipe makes 1 cocktail

The Lemon Drop Martini was created in the 1970s at Henry Africa's bar in San Francisco. The Lemon Drop falls into the category of cocktails we refer to as a "daisy," a sour-style drink made with any base spirit, liqueur, citrus juice, and sweetener. The flavor mimics the candy of the same name, and the sugar rim gives it a nice little candy-coated crunch. The key to an excellent Lemon Drop Martini is to make sure you are using fresh citrus juice and not overdoing it on the sweetener. A Lemon Drop should be tart!

CLASSIC LEMON DROP MARTINI	**RIFF** SKY–HIGH LEMON PIE	**N–A** LIFE'S LEMONS
GLASSWARE martini	**GLASSWARE** chilled coupe	**GLASSWARE** collins
Lemon wedge and sugar, for rim 2 ounces vodka ½ ounce orange liqueur 1 ounce fresh lemon juice 1 ounce Simple Syrup (page 26) Lemon twist, for garnish	1½ ounces citron vodka ½ ounce vanilla liqueur ½ ounce yuzu liqueur 1 ounce fresh lemon juice ¼ ounce Simple Syrup (page 26) 1 egg white Lemon twist, for garnish	1½ ounces Brewed Jasmine Tea (page 41) ½ ounce yuzu juice ½ fresh passion fruit seeds ½ ounce Honey Syrup (page 28) 3 ounces soda water Lemon wheel and passion fruit half, for garnish
Using a wedge of lemon, rim half of the outside of your martini glass and roll it in sugar. In a shaker tin, combine the vodka, orange liqueur, lemon juice, and simple syrup. Add cubed ice and shake vigorously for 12 seconds. Fine-strain into the sugar-rimmed martini glass and garnish with a lemon twist.	In a shaker tin, combine the citron vodka, vanilla liqueur, yuzu liqueur, lemon juice, simple syrup, and egg white. Dry shake (without ice) for 10 seconds. Open the shaker tin, add cubed ice, and shake again for another 12 seconds. Fine-strain into a chilled coupe and garnish with a lemon twist.	In a shaker tin, combine the jasmine tea, yuzu juice, passion fruit seeds, and honey syrup. Add cubed ice and shake vigorously for 10 seconds. Fine-strain into a collins glass over fresh ice and top with soda water. Gently stir to incorporate and garnish with a lemon wheel and passion fruit half.

PRO TIP Only rim half of your cocktail glass with sugar—that way it gives you the option to take a sip with or without the sugar.

LONDON CALLING

2002
Each recipe makes 1 cocktail

Chris Jepsen of famed London bar Milk & Honey created this citrus-forward gin drink that is layered with flavor. Fino sherry adds a touch of salinity and dries out the palate ever so slightly, bringing you back for more. This is a great introduction to the world of sherry and an absolute banger of a cocktail! For the variations of this drink, I wanted to introduce you to some other tasty-modifying spirits, such as Strega and akvavit. Both add a touch of anise in a complementary way without overpowering the drink.

CLASSIC LONDON CALLING	RIFF VANCOUVER CALLING	N–A COLD CALLING
GLASSWARE chilled Nick & Nora	**GLASSWARE** chilled coupe	**GLASSWARE** chilled Nick & Nora
1½ ounces dry gin ½ ounce fino sherry ½ ounce Rich Simple Syrup (page 26) ½ ounce fresh lemon juice 2 dashes orange bitters Grapefruit twist, for garnish	1 ounce pisco ½ ounce Liquore Strega or akvavit ½ ounce fino sherry ¾ ounce Acidified Grapefruit Juice (page 34) ¾ ounce Simple Syrup (page 26) 1 dash orange bitters Grapefruit twist, for garnish	1 ounce spirit-free gin 1 ounce nonalcoholic dry white wine ¾ ounce white cranberry juice ½ ounce Rich Simple Syrup (page 26) ½ ounce fresh lemon juice 1 dash orange bitters Lemon twist, for garnish
In a shaker tin, combine the gin, fino sherry, rich simple syrup, lemon juice, and orange bitters. Add cubed ice and shake vigorously for 12 seconds. Fine-strain into a chilled Nick & Nora glass and garnish with a grapefruit twist.	In a shaker tin, combine the pisco, Strega, fino sherry, acidified grapefruit juice, simple syrup, and orange bitters. Add cubed ice and shake vigorously for 12 seconds. Fine-strain into a chilled coupe and garnish with a grapefruit twist.	In a shaker tin, combine the spirit-free gin, nonalcoholic dry white wine, white cranberry juice, rich simple syrup, lemon juice, and orange bitters. Add cubed ice and shake vigorously for 10 seconds. Fine-strain into a chilled Nick & Nora and garnish with a lemon twist.

PRO TIP Sherry is a fortified wine. Once opened, you should store it in the fridge to slow the rate of oxidation.

Left to right: Vancouver Calling, London Calling, Cold Calling

Left to right: Miso Mai Tai,
Mai Tai, Tongue Tied

MAI TAI

1930s
Each recipe makes 1 cocktail

The mai tai is arguably one of the most famous tiki cocktails in the world, and it's probably the most butchered, too. A classic mai tai should never include orange or pineapple juice. The original recipe is meant to showcase the rums being used, not hide them behind a bunch of bottled juices. I like to keep my mai tai fairly traditional, but one way to get creative with it is to play around with the orgeat. For my variation I used a toasted sesame miso orgeat to add in an extra layer of flavor.

CLASSIC MAI TAI	RIFF MISO MAI TAI	N—A TONGUE TIED
GLASSWARE rocks	**GLASSWARE** rocks	**GLASSWARE** rocks
1½ ounces white rum ¾ ounce orange liqueur ½ ounce Orgeat (page 30) ¾ ounce fresh lime juice ½ ounce dark rum Mint sprig, for garnish	1 ounce overproof rum ½ ounce dark rum ½ ounce orange liqueur ½ ounce Toasted Sesame Miso Orgeat (page 30) ¾ ounce fresh lime juice 1 dash orange bitters Toasted sesame seeds, for garnish	1½ ounces spirit-free rum 1 ounce Acidified Orange Juice (page 34) ¾ ounce coconut water ½ ounce Orgeat (page 30) 2 dashes aromatic bitters Orange twist and fresh mint sprig, for garnish
In a shaker tin, combine the white rum, orange liqueur, orgeat, and lime juice. Add cubed ice and shake vigorously for 10 seconds. Strain into a rocks glass over pebble ice. Using the back of a bar spoon, carefully float the dark rum on top and garnish with a mint sprig.	In a shaker tin, combine the overproof rum, dark rum, orange liqueur, miso orgeat, lime juice, and orange bitters. Add cubed ice and shake vigorously for 12 seconds. Fine-strain into a rocks glass over pebble ice. Garnish with toasted sesame seeds.	In a shaker tin, combine the spirit-free rum, acidified orange juice, coconut water, orgeat, and aromatic bitters. Add cubed ice and shake vigorously for 10 seconds. Fine-strain into a rocks glass over fresh ice and garnish with an orange twist and mint sprig.

PRO TIP If you are allergic to almonds, try making an orgeat with another nut or seed. Cashews, pistachios, or even sunflower seeds all make tasty orgeats.

MANHATTAN

1880s
Each recipe makes 1 cocktail

The cheat code to this drink is right there in the name: Manhattan. This drink follows the 2-1-2 rule, which just happens to be the area code of Manhattan: 2 parts rye, 1 part sweet vermouth, 2 dashes bitters. The Manhattan is one of the most iconic cocktails, although it has sparked many variations. It is said to be one of the first "modern" cocktails because of its use of a fortified wine, vermouth. Although there is much debate on where and who created this cocktail, the original recipe has stayed much the same since its inception. No need to fix what isn't broken.

CLASSIC MANHATTAN	RIFF KUMBAYA	N—A AREA CODE 212
GLASSWARE chilled martini	GLASSWARE chilled coupe	GLASSWARE chilled Nick & Nora
2 ounces rye whiskey 1 ounce sweet vermouth 2 dashes Angostura bitters Cherry, for garnish	2 ounces Cedar-Smoked Rye (page 38) 1 ounce Amaro Montenegro 1 teaspoon Cinnamon Syrup (page 26) 2 dashes cherry cedar bitters Toasted marshmallow, for garnish	2 ounces spirit-free whiskey 1 ounce Lucano nonalcoholic amaro 1 teaspoon Falernum (page 30) 2 dashes aromatic bitters Orange twist, for garnish
In a mixing glass, combine the rye, sweet vermouth, and Angostura bitters. Add cubed ice and stir for no less than 30 rotations. Strain into a chilled martini glass and garnish with a cherry.	In a mixing glass, combine the cedar-smoked rye, Amaro Montenegro, cinnamon syrup, and cherry cedar bitters. Add cubed ice and stir for no less than 30 rotations. Strain into a chilled coupe and garnish with a toasted marshmallow.	In a mixing glass, combine the spirit-free whiskey, nonalcoholic amaro, falernum, and aromatic bitters. Add cubed ice and stir for no less than 30 rotations. Strain into a chilled Nick & Nora and garnish with an orange twist.

PRO TIP Rye in a Manhattan will provide a spicier note, whereas bourbon will be slightly sweeter. Feel free to interchange the two spirits or do a combination of both to satisfy your own palate.

Left to right: Kumbaya,
Manhattan, Area Code 212

Left to right: 1,000 Yellow Daisies,
Milk Marg, Margarita

MARGARITA

1940s
Each recipe makes 1 cocktail

Called a Tequila Daisy, Picador, Tequila Sour, and finally, as we know it today, the Margarita, this is hands down my favorite cocktail. The combination of tequila, orange liqueur, and fresh citrus work in harmony with one another to really highlight all the ingredients' best qualities. For me a salt rim is a must, and I always want it served on the rocks. But that's just a personal preference. Like many classic cocktails, there is much debate on who and where the first margarita was created. But I think a bit of mystery makes the drink that much better. Served up, on the rocks, or blended, drink it how you like it!

CLASSIC MARGARITA	**RIFF** MILK MARG	**N-A** 1,000 YELLOW DAISIES
GLASSWARE rocks	**GLASSWARE** rocks	**GLASSWARE** chilled coupe
Lime wedge and salt, for rim 2 ounces blanco tequila ½ ounce orange liqueur 1 ounce fresh lime juice ½ ounce Agave Syrup (page 25) Lime wheel, for garnish	Lime wedge and salt, for rim 1½ ounces blanco tequila ¾ ounce Milk Liqueur (page 39) ½ ounce Vanilla Bean Syrup (page 27) 1 ounce fresh lime juice Orange twist, for garnish	2 ounces spirit-free tequila 1 ounce Acidified Orange Juice (page 34) ¾ ounce Vanilla Bean Syrup (page 27) 2 dashes orange bitters 2 drops Saline Solution (page 40) 1 egg white Edible flower, for garnish
Using a wedge of lime, rim half of the outside of your rocks glass and roll it in salt. In a shaker tin, combine the tequila, orange liqueur, lime juice, and agave syrup. Add cubed ice and shake vigorously for 12 seconds. Strain into the salt-rimmed rocks glass over fresh ice. Garnish with a lime wheel.	Using a wedge of lime, rim half of the outside of your rocks glass and roll it in salt. In a shaker tin, combine the tequila, milk liqueur, vanilla bean syrup, and lime juice. Add cubed ice and shake vigorously for 12 seconds. Strain into your salt-rimmed rocks glass over fresh ice. Garnish with an orange twist.	In a shaker tin, combine the spirit-free tequila, acidified orange juice, vanilla bean syrup, orange bitters, saline solution, and egg white. Dry shake (without ice) for 10 seconds. Open the shaker tin, add cubed ice, and shake again for another 12 seconds. Fine-strain into a chilled coupe and garnish with an edible flower.

 PRO TIP Use a good-quality salt, something like a flaky sea salt, for the rim of your glass. And be sure to roll just the outside of your glass in the salt, to avoid getting too much salt in your drink.

MOJITO

1930s
Each recipe makes 1 cocktail

The mojito's roots can be traced back to the sixteenth century. Back then it was known as El Draque, and it was made with aguardiente, a cane spirit that predates rum. It wasn't until the 1930s that the mojito first showed up in print. It's a Cuban cocktail through and through, best enjoyed with a light-style Cuban rum, or whatever you can get your hands on. One way you can make a mojito your own is by adding some fresh fruit. Give the Kiwito a try or swap in your favorite fruit instead.

CLASSIC MOJITO	RIFF KIWITO	N—A MANJITO
GLASSWARE collins	**GLASSWARE** rocks	**GLASSWARE** collins
2 ounces light rum	1 ounce cachaça	¼ mango
¾ ounce fresh lime juice	1 ounce rhum agricole	4 or 5 fresh mint leaves
½ ounce Simple Syrup (page 26)	½ fresh kiwi	½ ounce fresh lime juice
5 or 6 fresh mint leaves	½ ounce fresh lime juice	½ ounce Rich Simple Syrup (page 26)
2 ounces soda water	3 fresh mint leaves	3 ounces sparkling coconut water
Lime wedge and mint sprig, for garnish	2 teaspoons raw sugar	Mango slice and mint sprig, for garnish
	Fresh kiwi slice and mint sprig, for garnish	
In a shaker tin, combine the light rum, lime juice, simple syrup, and mint leaves. Add cubed ice and shake vigorously for 10 seconds. Fine-strain into a collins glass over cracked ice and top with soda water. Gently stir to incorporate and garnish with a lime wedge and mint sprig.	In a shaker tin, combine the cachaça, rhum agricole, kiwi, lime juice, mint leaves, and raw sugar. Gently muddle the kiwi, just to break it up. Add cubed ice and shake vigorously for 10 seconds. Fine-strain into a rocks glass over fresh ice and garnish with a kiwi slice and mint sprig.	In a shaker tin, combine the mango, mint leaves, lime juice, and rich simple syrup. Add cubed ice and shake vigorously for 10 seconds. "Dirty dump" the entire contents of the shaker tin into a collins glass and top with sparkling coconut water. Give a gentle stir to incorporate and garnish with a mango slice and mint sprig.

PRO TIP Keep the leaves of your mint on the stems when making your mojito. The stems are jam-packed full of flavor. Or save them to make a simple syrup.

Kiwito

Navy Grog

NAVY GROG

1940s
Each recipe makes 1 cocktail

I hope you've got your sea legs, because this is a bit of a boozy one. The navy grog is a combination of three different styles of rum, and it is meant to showcase how well rums blend together. Sweetened by honey for even more depth of flavor, the navy grog is easy to make, but I would suggest limiting yourself to just one. Okay, maybe two.

CLASSIC NAVY GROG	RIFF ROCKY WATERS	N—A SMOOTH SAILING
GLASSWARE rocks	**GLASSWARE** collins	**GLASSWARE** rocks
1 ounce dark rum 1 ounce gold rum 1 ounce white rum 1 ounce Honey Syrup (page 28) ¾ ounce grapefruit juice ¾ ounce lime juice ¾ ounce soda water Garnish with mint sprig and lime wheel	1 ounce rhum agricole 1 ounce aged cachaça ½ ounce light rum ¾ ounce grapefruit juice ½ ounce yuzu juice ½ ounce Ginger Honey Syrup (page 28) 1 ounce ginger beer Garnish with mint sprig and candied ginger	2 ounces spirit-free rum ¾ ounce Falernum (page 30) ¾ ounce grapefruit juice ½ ounce lime juice ½ ounce Ginger Honey Syrup (page 28) 2 dashes aromatic bitters 1 ounce ginger beer Garnish with a cinnamon-dusted grapefruit wedge
In a shaker tin, combine the three rums, honey syrup, grapefruit, and lime juice. Add cubed ice and vigorously shake for 10 seconds. Single strain into a rocks glass over pebble ice and top with soda water. Garnish with a mint sprig and lime wheel.	In a shaker tin, combine rhum agricole, aged cachaça, light rum, grapefruit juice, yuzu juice, and ginger honey syrup. Add cubed ice and vigorously shake for 10 seconds. Fine-strain into a collins glass over fresh ice and top with ginger beer. Give a gentle mix to incorporate. Garnish with a mint sprig and candied ginger.	In a shaker tin, combine spirit-free rum, falernum, grapefruit juice, lime juice, ginger honey syrup, and aromatic bitters. Add cubed ice and vigorously shake for 10 seconds. Single-strain into a rocks glass over fresh ice and top with ginger beer. Garnish with a cinnamon-dusted grapefruit wedge.

PRO TIP To make your own pebble or crushed ice at home, fill a clean pillowcase with cubed ice and whack it with a mallet or muddler. Then store your crushed ice in a ziplock bag in the freezer for when you need it.

NEGRONI

20th Century
Each recipe makes 1 cocktail

The Negroni is an essential three-ingredient classic cocktail, and you either love it or hate it. It's said to be first served at Caffè Casoni in Florence, Italy, and named after Count Camilo Negroni. It has spawned countless variations, and you can order one at just about any bar in the world. It is boozy, bitter, and bold. Typically made in equal parts, the Negroni relies heavily on the gin you choose and the vermouth you pair it with. Campari is always a staple in the classic recipe, but feel free to play around with other aperitifs when it comes to crafting your own. The High & Dry is one of my favorite variations I've come up with on the Negroni. It is an excellent "starter" Negroni for those who might find the original a bit too bold.

CLASSIC NEGRONI	RIFF HIGH & DRY	N—A NO-GRONI
GLASSWARE rocks	**GLASSWARE** rocks	**GLASSWARE** rocks
1 ounce gin 1 ounce sweet vermouth 1 ounce Campari Orange twist, for garnish	¾ ounce gin ¾ ounce elderflower liqueur ¾ ounce Campari 3 drops orange blossom water 2 ounces cava or other dry sparkling wine Grapefruit slice, for garnish	1½ ounces spirit-free gin ½ ounce Wilfred's nonalcoholic aperitif 1½ ounces Stappi Red Bitter soda 1½ ounces soda water Orange slice and rosemary sprig, for garnish
In a mixing glass, combine the gin, sweet vermouth, and Campari. Add cubed ice and stir for no less than 30 rotations. Strain into a rocks glass over one large piece of ice. Garnish with an orange twist.	In a mixing glass, combine the gin, elderflower liqueur, Campari, and orange blossom water. Add cubed ice and stir for 15 rotations. Strain into a rocks glass over fresh ice and top with cava. Gently stir to incorporate and garnish with a grapefruit slice.	In an ice-filled rocks glass, combine the spirit-free gin, Wilfred's nonalcoholic aperitif, Stappi Red Bitter, and soda water. Gently stir to incorporate and garnish with a slice of orange and rosemary sprig.

PRO TIP The Negroni is an equal-parts drink, so it's really easy to make in a large batch and store in your freezer. When you're ready to serve, just pour 3 ounces over ice and give it a quick stir.

Left to right: Negroni, No-Groni, High & Dry

Cereal Milk Punch

NEW ORLEANS MILK PUNCH

1940s
Each recipe makes 1 cocktail

A much lighter version of eggnog, the New Orleans milk punch got its start at Brennan's, an iconic restaurant in the French Quarter. Some would say it's a brunch drink while others claim it to be an after-dinner drink. No matter what time of day, it's simply delicious. If brandy isn't your spirit of choice, swap it out with bourbon like I did for the Cereal Milk Punch or use your favorite dark spirit.

CLASSIC NEW ORLEANS MILK PUNCH	RIFF CEREAL MILK PUNCH	N-A 2%
GLASSWARE rocks	**GLASSWARE** rocks	**GLASSWARE** rocks
2 ounces brandy 3 ounces whole milk 1 ounce Simple Syrup (page 26) 2 dashes vanilla extract Grated nutmeg, for garnish	2 ounces bourbon ½ ounce oloroso sherry 2 ounces Cereal Milk (page 38) ½ ounce Vanilla Bean Simple Syrup (page 27) Dry cereal, for garnish	2 ounces Brewed Lapsang Souchong Tea (page 41) 2 ounces almond milk ½ ounce Cinnamon Syrup (page 26) Grated cinnamon, for garnish
In a shaker tin, combine the brandy, milk, simple syrup, and vanilla extract. Add cubed ice and shake vigorously for 7 seconds. Strain into a rocks glass over one large piece of ice and garnish with grated nutmeg.	In a shaker tin, combine the bourbon, oloroso sherry, cereal milk, and vanilla bean syrup. Add cubed ice and shake vigorously for 7 seconds. Strain into a rocks glass over one large piece of ice and garnish with cereal.	In a shaker tin, combine the lapsang souchong tea, almond milk, and cinnamon syrup. Add cubed ice and shake vigorously for 7 seconds. Single-strain into a rocks glass over one large piece of ice and garnish with grated cinnamon.

PRO TIP If avoiding dairy, use a dairy-free option that is higher in fat. Coconut milk, for example, will still give you that desired body you want from this drink.

NEW YORK SOUR

1870s
Each recipe makes 1 cocktail

First appearing in print in 1934 as the New York Sour, this drink has gone through several names: the Continental Sour, Southern Sour, Claret Snap, and Brunswick Sour. The New York Sour is just an extension of the whiskey sour with the addition of a red wine float. The wine provides additional aromatics, gives off a fruitiness, and adds a pop of color. You can add a red wine float to many other sour-style cocktails. If added to a margarita, it's called a Devil's Margarita.

CLASSIC NEW YORK SOUR	RIFF SANGRIA SOUR	N—A SOHO SOUR
GLASSWARE rocks	**GLASSWARE** chilled coupe	**GLASSWARE** chilled sour glass
2 ounces bourbon or rye whiskey 1 ounce fresh lemon juice ¾ ounce Simple Syrup (page 26) 1 egg white ½ ounce dry red wine Lemon twist and Angostura bitters, for garnish	1½ ounces rye whiskey ½ ounce amaretto ¾ ounce Blackberry Syrup (page 26) 1 ounce Acidified Orange Juice (page 34) 1 egg white ¾ ounce Lambrusco (sparkling red wine) Lemon twist, for garnish	2 ounces Brewed Assam Tea (page 41) ¾ ounce Falernum (page 30) ¾ ounce fresh lemon juice 1 orange peel 2 dashes aromatic bitters 1 egg white ½ ounce nonalcoholic red wine Lemon twist and grated nutmeg, for garnish
In a shaker tin, combine the bourbon, lemon juice, simple syrup, and egg white. Dry shake (without ice) for 10 seconds. Open the shaker tin, add cubed ice, and shake again for another 12 seconds. Fine-strain into a rocks glass. Using the back of a bar spoon, carefully layer the red wine on top. Garnish with a lemon twist and a few drops of Angostura bitters.	In a shaker tin, combine the rye, amaretto, blackberry syrup, acidified orange juice, and egg white. Dry shake (without ice) for 10 seconds. Open the shaker tin, add cubed ice, and shake again for another 12 seconds. Fine-strain into a chilled coupe glass. Using the back of a bar spoon, carefully layer the Lambrusco on top. Garnish with a lemon twist.	In a shaker tin, combine the Assam tea, falernum, lemon juice, orange peel, aromatic bitters, and egg white. Dry shake (without ice) for 10 seconds. Open the shaker tin, add cubed ice, and shake again for another 12 seconds. Fine-strain into a chilled sour glass. Using the back of a bar spoon, carefully layer the nonalcoholic red wine on top. Garnish with a lemon twist and grated nutmeg.

PRO TIP When "floating" red wine on a cocktail, make sure you are pouring the wine as close to the surface as possible, with a slow and steady hand. This will help keep the layers separated, giving you that clear visual divide between the cocktail and wine.

Left to right: Sangria Sour,
New York Sour, Soho Sour

Florida Old-Fashioned

OLD-FASHIONED

1700s
Each recipe makes 1 cocktail

The old-fashioned is the ultimate definition of a cocktail: spirit, sugar, bitters, and water. It is not so much a drink as it is a template to follow. In its early years it was known simply as a Whiskey Cocktail: a portion of whiskey with a few dashes of bitters. As time went on, more was added to the whiskey cocktail. So when people just wanted their whiskey with bitters, they would ask for the "old-fashioned" cocktail. Using the old-fashioned as a template, the combinations are endless. Swap out the bourbon for mezcal or rum. Change your sugar to maple syrup. Instead of aromatic bitters, why not use chocolate or spruce. Have fun with it and make it your own.

CLASSIC OLD-FASHIONED	RIFF FLORIDA OLD-FASHIONED	N—A CALL ME OLD-FASHIONED
GLASSWARE rocks	GLASSWARE rocks	GLASSWARE rocks
1 raw sugar cube 2 dashes Angostura bitters 2 ounces bourbon Orange twist, for garnish	1 grapefruit wedge 2 ounces bourbon ¼ ounce amaretto ¼ ounce Rich Simple Syrup (page 26) 2 dashes orange bitters 2 dashes Angostura bitters Grapefruit wedge, for garnish	2 ounces Brewed Lapsang Souchong Tea (page 41) ½ ounce maple syrup 1 orange peel 2 dashes aromatic bitters Orange twist and cherry, for garnish
Add a raw sugar cube and Angostura bitters to a mixing glass. Gently muddle to break down the sugar cube and form a paste-like consistency. Add the bourbon and cubed ice to the mixing glass and stir no less than 30 rotations. Strain into a rocks glass over a single large piece of ice. Garnish with an orange twist.	Add a wedge of grapefruit to a mixing glass. Gently muddle the grapefruit, just enough to release the juices. Add the bourbon, amaretto, rich simple syrup, orange bitters, and Angostura bitters to the same mixing glass. Add cubed ice and stir for no less than 30 rotations. Strain into a rocks glass over fresh ice. Garnish with a grapefruit wedge.	In a mixing glass, combine the lapsang souchong tea, maple syrup, orange peel, and aromatic bitters. Add cubed ice and stir for no less than 30 rotations. Strain into a rocks glass over fresh ice and garnish with an orange twist and a cherry.

PRO TIP Your old-fashioned is only going to be as good as the ingredients you use. If you wouldn't sip the spirit neat, then don't use it in your drink.

PALOMA

1950s
Each recipe makes 1 cocktail

If I were to ask you what the national drink of Mexico was, your first guess would probably be the margarita. But that would be wrong; it is in fact the Paloma. The refreshing three-ingredient drink requires no fancy bar equipment and is built right in the glass. It is typically made with a blanco tequila, but you can swap that out for a reposado or even mezcal. Some like to salt the rim, others like it directly in the glass, or none at all. The origins of the Paloma are a mystery, but it is often credited to Don Javier Delgado Corona, former owner of La Capilla in Tequila, Mexico, who is also responsible for creating the Batanga.

CLASSIC PALOMA	RIFF TEXAS DOVE	N—A PIGEON–TOED
GLASSWARE collins	**GLASSWARE** collins	**GLASSWARE** collins
2 ounces blanco tequila ½ ounce fresh lime juice Pinch of salt 4 ounces grapefruit soda Grapefruit wedge, for garnish	Wedge of lime and Tajín, for rim 1 ounce blanco tequila ½ ounce mezcal ½ ounce Aperol 1 ounce Acidified Grapefruit Juice (page 34) ½ ounce Rosemary Syrup (page 27) 3 ounces soda water Lime wheel and rosemary sprig, for garnish	2 ounces spirit-free tequila 1½ ounces fresh grapefruit juice ½ ounce fresh lime juice ½ ounce Ginger Honey Syrup (page 28) 1 grapefruit wedge 1-inch piece fresh ginger 2 ounces soda water Candied ginger, for garnish
In an ice-filled collins glass, combine the tequila, lime juice, pinch of salt, and grapefruit soda. Gently stir to incorporate and garnish with a grapefruit wedge.	Using a wedge of lime, rim half of the outside of your collins glass and roll it in Tajín. In a shaker tin, combine the tequila, mezcal, Aperol, acidified grapefruit juice, and rosemary syrup. Add cubed ice and shake vigorously for 7 seconds. Fine-strain into your Tajín-rimmed collins glass and top with soda water. Gently stir to incorporate and garnish with a lime wheel and rosemary sprig.	In a shaker tin, combine the spirit-free tequila, grapefruit juice, lime juice, ginger honey syrup, wedge of grapefruit, and fresh ginger. Gently muddle the grapefruit and ginger, just enough to break them up. Add cubed ice and shake vigorously for 10 seconds. Fine-strain into a collins glass over fresh ice and top with soda water. Gently stir to incorporate and garnish with candied ginger.

PRO TIP   If you can't find grapefruit soda, use fresh grapefruit juice and soda water as a replacement.

Left to right: Paloma, Texas Dove, Pigeon-Toed

Bottom left: Motion Sickness, *top left:* Antihero, *right:* Paper Plane

PAPER PLANE

2008
Each recipe makes 1 cocktail

Named after the popular 2000s song by M.I.A., the Paper Plane is a riff on the classic cocktail, The Last Word, and was created by award-winning bartender Sam Ross. The Last Word is an equal-parts cocktail, as is the Paper Plane. They both play with the balance of sour, herbal, and bitterness. The flavors work in harmony with one another to create a modern-day classic. My variations also follow the equal-parts rule, using the template of base spirit, herbal liqueur, and bitterness, and are also named after some current popular songs of the 2020s.

CLASSIC PAPER PLANE	RIFF ANTIHERO	N—A MOTION SICKNESS
GLASSWARE chilled Nick & Nora	**GLASSWARE** chilled Nick & Nora	**GLASSWARE** rocks glass
¾ ounce bourbon ¾ ounce Aperol ¾ ounce Amaro Nonino ¾ ounce fresh lemon juice Lemon twist, for garnish	¾ ounce rhum agricole ¾ ounce Liquore Strega ¾ ounce orange liqueur ¾ ounce fresh lime juice 2 sage leaves 3 drops Saline Solution (page 40) Sage leaf, for garnish	¾ ounce Brewed Assam Tea (page 41) ¾ ounce Lucano nonalcoholic amaro ¾ ounce Martini Torino Vibrante nonalcoholic aperitif ¾ ounce fresh lemon juice Lemon wheel, for garnish
In a shaker tin, combine the bourbon, Aperol, Amaro Nonino, and lemon juice. Add cubed ice and shake vigorously for 12 seconds. Fine-strain into a chilled Nick & Nora glass and garnish with a lemon twist.	In a shaker tin, combine the rhum agricole, Strega, orange liqueur, lime juice, sage leaves, and saline solution. Add cubed ice and shake vigorously for 12 seconds. Fine-strain into a chilled Nick & Nora glass and garnish with a sage leaf.	In a shaker tin, combine the Assam black tea, Lucano nonalcoholic amaro, Torino Vibrante, and lemon juice. Add cubed ice and shake vigorously for 10 seconds. Fine-strain into a rocks glass and garnish with a lemon wheel.

PRO TIP The original Paper Plane recipe calls for Amaro Nonino, specifically. If you are unable to find Nonino, a good replacement is Amaro Montenegro.

PENICILLIN

2000s
Each recipe makes 1 cocktail

Here's another Sam Ross original. Created at Milk & Honey in New York City, the Penicillin is actually a riff on a Gold Rush. This one uses blended Scotch and ginger as the defining flavor components. It's an excellent introductory cocktail into the world of blended Scotch. The flavors are tart, spicy, and a touch on the smoky side with the addition of an Islay float. Both variations pay homage to the "smoky" elements of the original, but by using mezcal and Lapsang Souchong tea in place of the Scotch.

CLASSIC PENICILLIN	RIFF SMOKESTACK LIGHTNING	N-A LOVESICK
GLASSWARE rocks	**GLASSWARE** rocks	**GLASSWARE** heatproof glass
2 ounces blended Scotch ¾ ounce Ginger Honey Syrup (page 28) ¾ ounce fresh lemon juice ¼ ounce Islay single-malt Scotch Candied ginger, for garnish	1½ ounces white whiskey ½ ounce mezcal ½ ounce ginger liqueur ¾ ounce Black Pepper Honey Syrup (page 28) ¾ ounce fresh lemon juice Lemon twist, for garnish	4 ounces freshly Brewed Lapsang Souchong Tea (page 41) ¾ ounce Ginger Honey Syrup (page 28) ½ ounce fresh lemon juice 2-inch piece fresh ginger 3 black peppercorns Lemon wheel, for garnish
In a shaker tin, combine the blended Scotch, ginger honey syrup, and lemon juice. Add cubed ice and shake vigorously for 12 seconds. Strain into a rocks glass over fresh ice and carefully pour the Islay Scotch on top as a float. Garnish with candied ginger.	In a shaker tin, combine the white whiskey, mezcal, ginger liqueur, black pepper honey syrup, and lemon juice. Add cubed ice and shake vigorously for 12 seconds. Fine-strain into a rocks glass over fresh ice and garnish with a lemon twist.	In a heatproof glass, combine the lapsang souchong tea, ginger honey syrup, lemon juice, fresh ginger, and black peppercorns. Gently stir to incorporate and garnish with a lemon wheel.

 PRO TIP If you don't want to make the ginger honey syrup, muddle a piece of fresh ginger into your cocktail and use a basic honey syrup to sweeten.

Left to right: Penicillin, Lovesick, Smokestack Lightning

Left to right: Diced Pineapples, Tepache Colada, Piña Colada

PIÑA COLADA

1950s
Each recipe makes 1 cocktail

The Piña Colada, created by Ramón "Monchito" Marrero at the Caribe Hilton Hotel in Puerto Rico, is one of the most underrated cocktails out there. It is also one of the most butchered. If you're using quality ingredients, it shouldn't be overly sweet or taste like suntan lotion. Fun fact: The Diced Pineapples variation is one of the drinks that helped me win the title of World's Best Bartender.

`CLASSIC` PIÑA COLADA	`RIFF` DICED PINEAPPLES	`N—A` TEPACHE COLADA
GLASSWARE hurricane glass	**GLASSWARE** rocks	**GLASSWARE** rocks
2 ounces white rum 1½ ounces cream of coconut 1½ ounces pineapple juice ½ ounce fresh lime juice Pineapple wedge and leaf, for garnish	1½ ounces gin ½ ounce Junmai Nama Nigori Sake 1 ounce Pineapple Kasu (page 40) ½ ounce Pineapple Gomme Syrup (page 29) ¾ ounce fresh lime juice 3 drops Saline Solution (page 40) 1 dash tiki bitters Grated black lime and pineapple leaf, for garnish	2 ounces Tepache (page 40) 1 ounce pineapple juice ½ ounce fresh lime juice 1½ ounces cream of coconut Grated nutmeg and pineapple leaf, for garnish
In a shaker tin, combine the white rum, cream of coconut, pineapple juice, and lime juice. Add ½ cup of pebble ice and whip shake (see Pro Tip on page 168) until the ice has melted. Strain into a hurricane glass over pebble ice and garnish with a pineapple wedge and leaf.	In a shaker tin, combine the gin, Nigori sake, pineapple kasu, pineapple gomme syrup, lime juice, saline solution, and tiki bitters. Add cubed ice and shake vigorously for 12 seconds. Fine-strain into a rocks glass over fresh ice and garnish with grated black lime and a pineapple leaf.	In a rocks glass, combine the tepache, pineapple juice, lime juice, and cream of coconut. Add pebble or crushed ice to fill half the glass. With a swizzle stick or bar spoon, swizzle (see Pro Tip on page 73) the liquid and ice together for 5 seconds. Add more pebble ice to fill the remainder of the glass. Swizzle again for another 5 seconds. Remove the swizzle stick and top the glass with more pebble ice. Garnish with grated nutmeg and pineapple leaf.

PRO TIP Make sure you are using a full-fat cream of coconut (not coconut milk or low-fat coconut cream).

PORN STAR MARTINI

2000s

Each recipe makes 1 cocktail, except for Clearly Naked Highball, which makes 4 cocktails

This cocktail does not resemble a martini in any way, shape, or form, but the combination of vanilla and passion fruit is undeniably flavorful. It was originally called the Maverick Martini but is now better known as the Porn Star Martini. Why the change in name? Your guess is as good as mine. It was created at London's Townhouse bar by Douglas Ankrah. You are meant to sip your martini and chase it with a small pour of sparkling wine. For my variations I wanted to go a little outside the box while still staying true to the original. Clarifying and carbonating the cocktail changes the overall texture and mouthfeel, making it more refreshing.

CLASSIC PORN STAR MARTINI	RIFF CLEARLY NAKED HIGHBALL	N—A PARENTAL ADVISORY SOUR
GLASSWARE chilled martini and shot glass	GLASSWARE 4 highballs	GLASSWARE chilled coupe
1½ ounces vanilla vodka ½ ounce passion fruit liqueur 1 ounce passion fruit puree ½ ounce fresh lime juice ½ ounce Vanilla Bean Syrup (page 27) Fresh passion fruit half, for garnish 2 ounces sparkling wine	4 ounces vanilla vodka 4 ounces coconut vodka 2 ounces ginger liqueur 4 ounces passion fruit puree 2 ounces fresh lime juice 2 ounces Vanilla Bean Syrup (page 27) 4 ounces whole milk 12 ounces sparkling wine 4 fresh passion fruit halves, for garnish	2 ounces spirit-free gin ½ ounce Martini Torino Vibrante nonalcoholic aperitif 1 ounce passion fruit puree ¾ ounce fresh lime juice ¾ ounce Vanilla Bean Syrup (page 27) 1 egg white Lime twist, for garnish
In a shaker tin, combine the vanilla vodka, passion fruit liqueur, passion fruit puree, lime juice, and vanilla bean syrup. Add cubed ice and shake vigorously for 12 seconds. Fine-strain into a chilled martini glass. Garnish with the passion fruit half and serve with a side of sparkling wine.	In a large container, combine the vanilla vodka, coconut vodka, ginger liqueur, passion fruit puree, lime juice, and vanilla bean syrup. In a small saucepan, heat the milk over medium-low heat. Once the milk has come to a simmer, remove from the heat and combine with the vodka mixture. Do not stir.	In a shaker tin, combine the spirit-free gin, Martini Vibrante, passion fruit puree, lime juice, vanilla bean syrup, and egg white. Dry shake (without ice) for 10 seconds. Open the shaker tin, add cubed ice, and shake again for another 12 seconds. Fine-strain into a chilled coupe glass and garnish with a lime twist.

Place the mix in the fridge, uncovered, and let sit for 3 to 4 hours (or longer). The mix should naturally separate.

Once the mix has settled, carefully and slowly strain it through a coffee filter or tight-weave cheesecloth into a clean container, until the mix is clear. To ensure a crystal-clear finish, do not rush the straining process. You may need to filter it two or three times.

Bottle and refrigerate the highball mix until you are ready to serve.

To serve 1 drink, pour 4 ounces of the highball mix into a highball glass over fresh ice and top with 3 ounces sparkling wine. Gently stir to incorporate and garnish with a fresh passion fruit half.

PRO TIP If you don't want to buy an entire bottle of vanilla vodka for just one drink, you can easily make your own with vodka and vanilla bean pods. Pour a portion of vodka into a clean mason jar and add a vanilla bean pod that has been split down the middle lengthwise. Let sit at room temperature for 24 hours and enjoy.

Left to right: Parental Advisory Sour, Clearly Naked Highball, Porn Star Martini

Ramos Gin Fizz

RAMOS GIN FIZZ

1888
Each recipe makes 1 cocktail

The Ramos Gin Fizz is the cocktail every bartender loves to hate. Created by Henry Charles "Carl" Ramos at the Imperial Cabinet Saloon in New Orleans, the Ramos Gin Fizz was originally intended to be shaken for 12 to 15 minutes straight. Ramos hired an entire team of "shaker men" just to keep up with the demand. Today, you can get away with shaking a Ramos for far less time: 2 minutes max should do the trick.

CLASSIC RAMOS GIN FIZZ

GLASSWARE chilled collins

2 ounces gin
¾ ounce Simple Syrup (page 26)
½ ounce heavy cream
½ ounce fresh lemon juice
½ ounce fresh lime juice
3 dashes orange blossom water
1 egg white
2½ ounces soda water
Lemon twist, for garnish

In a shaker tin, combine the gin, simple syrup, heavy cream, lemon juice, lime juice, orange blossom water, and egg white. Add ½ cup of pebble or crushed ice and whip shake until the ice has completely melted. Pour half the contents into a chilled collins glass. Place the collins glass back into the freezer for 2 minutes to allow the cocktail to settle. Then pour the remainder into the collins glass and slowly add the soda water. Add a straw and garnish with a lemon twist.

RIFF NORDIC GIN FIZZ

GLASSWARE chilled collins

1 ounce gin
1 ounce akvavit
1 tablespoon plain Greek yogurt
¾ ounce fresh lemon juice
½ ounce fresh grapefruit juice
½ ounce Rich Simple Syrup (page 26)
3 dashes rose water
1 egg white
2½ ounces soda water
Mist of absinthe, for garnish

In a shaker tin, combine the gin, akvavit, yogurt, lemon juice, grapefruit juice, rich simple syrup, rose water, and egg white. Add ½ cup of pebble ice and whip shake until the ice has completely melted. Pour half the contents into a chilled collins glass. Place the collins glass back into the freezer for 2 minutes to allow the cocktail to settle. Then pour the remainder into the collins glass and slowly add the soda water. Add a straw and garnish with a mist of absinthe.

N—A JULIUS GINLESS FIZZ

GLASSWARE chilled collins

1½ ounces spirit-free gin
1 ounce heavy cream
1 teaspoon marmalade
1 ounce Acidified Orange Juice (page 34)
¾ ounce Vanilla Bean Syrup (page 27)
1 egg white
2 ounces soda water
Orange twist, for garnish

In a shaker tin, combine the spirit-free gin, heavy cream, marmalade, acidified orange juice, vanilla bean syrup, and egg white. Add ½ cup of pebble ice and whip shake until the ice has completely melted. Pour half the contents into a chilled collins glass. Place the collins glass back into the freezer for 2 minutes to allow the cocktail to settle. Then pour the remainder into the collins glass and slowly add the soda water. Add a straw and garnish with an orange twist.

ROSITA

1970s
Each recipe makes 1 cocktail

The Rosita is considered a modern-day classic, though its history is a little murky. It was supposedly created by bartending legend Gaz Regan, but even he forgot that he once came up with the drink. It is more akin to the style of a "Perfect" Negroni, meaning that it utilizes both dry and sweet vermouth. It is an excellent cocktail to try if you are both a tequila lover and spirit-forward drinker. El Saguaro plays with that "perfect" template, but by using two other fortified spirits, sherry and elderflower liqueur, whereas the spirit-free variation brings a complementary coffee flavor to the bold bitterness of the Rosita.

CLASSIC ROSITA	**RIFF EL SAGUARO**	**N—A COFFEE WITH ROSA**
GLASSWARE rocks	**GLASSWARE** rocks	**GLASSWARE** rocks
1½ ounces reposado tequila ½ ounce sweet vermouth ½ ounce dry vermouth ½ ounce Campari 1 dash Angostura bitters Lemon twist, for garnish	1½ ounces blanco tequila ½ ounce fino sherry ½ ounce elderflower liqueur 3 drops Saline Solution (page 40) 1 dash orange bitters Lemon twist and nori sheet, for garnish	1½ ounces spirit-free tequila ½ ounce Martini Torino Vibrante nonalcoholic aperitif 2 ounces Stappi Red Bitter soda 2 tablespoons coffee beans 3 coffee beans and orange twist, for garnish
In a mixing glass, combine the tequila, sweet vermouth, dry vermouth, Campari, and Angostura bitters. Add cubed ice and stir for no less than 30 rotations. Strain into a rocks glass over one large piece of ice. Garnish with a lemon twist.	In a mixing glass, combine the tequila, fino sherry, elderflower liqueur, saline solution, and orange bitters. Add cubed ice and stir for no less than 30 rotations. Strain into a rocks glass over one large piece of ice. Garnish with a lemon twist and sheet of nori.	In a mixing glass, combine the spirit-free tequila, Martini Vibrante, Stappi Red Bitter, and 2 tablespoons coffee beans. Add cubed ice and stir for no less than 15 rotations. Fine-strain into a rocks glass over one large piece of ice. Garnish with 3 coffee beans and an orange twist.

PRO TIP Think Negroni variations as a template—spirit, bitter, sweet—and then start to experiment with different combinations. There are so many possibilities!

Bottom: Rosita, *top:* Coffee with Rosa, *right:* El Saguaro

Bottom: BJ on the PJ, *top:* Sandy Cheeks, *right:* Sex on the Beach

SEX ON THE BEACH

1980s
Each recipe makes 1 cocktail

Created by Florida bartender Ted Pizio, the name alone is enough to grab anyone's attention. There is nothing "craft" about this cocktail; it is a quintessential late eighties/early nineties–style of drink. It's a mash-up of a Fuzzy Navel and Cape Cod, two popular drinks at that time. A touch on the sweeter side, this one is fairly refreshing when made properly. It's a drink you are likely to find at any poolside cabana or big chain restaurant. Since the original name is so "cheeky," I took it upon myself to be just as playful with the variations names. BJ on the PJ: a soon to be modern-day classic cocktail!

CLASSIC SEX ON THE BEACH	RIFF SANDY CHEEKS	N–A BJ ON THE PJ
GLASSWARE collins	**GLASSWARE** collins	**GLASSWARE** collins
1½ ounces vodka ½ ounce peach schnapps ½ ounce crème de cassis 1½ ounces fresh orange juice 1½ ounces unsweetened cranberry juice Paper cocktail umbrella, for garnish	1½ ounces coconut vodka ½ ounce melon liqueur ½ ounce orange liqueur 1½ ounces pineapple juice ½ ounce fresh lime juice Toasted coconut flakes, for garnish	1½ ounces lychee juice 1½ ounces mango juice 1½ ounces coconut water ½ ounce fresh lime juice ½ ounce Simple Syrup (page 26) Mango slice, for garnish
In a shaker tin, combine the vodka, peach schnapps, crème de cassis, orange juice, and cranberry juice. Add cubed ice and shake vigorously for 10 seconds. Strain into a collins glass over fresh ice and garnish with an umbrella.	In a shaker tin, combine the coconut vodka, melon liqueur, orange liqueur, pineapple juice, and lime juice. Add cubed ice and shake vigorously for 10 seconds. Strain into a collins glass over fresh ice and garnish with toasted coconut flakes.	In a shaker tin, combine the lychee juice, mango juice, coconut water, lime juice, and simple syrup. Add cubed ice and shake vigorously for 10 seconds. Strain into a collins glass and garnish with a mango slice.

PRO TIP Using freshly squeezed, unsweetened juices will always give you more control over the final result of a cocktail. It is much easier to manage the sweetness of a drink when it is not already in your mixers.

SIDECAR

1920s
Each recipe makes 1 cocktail

Arguably the most famous classic Cognac cocktail, the Sidecar is a simple three-ingredient drink that relies heavily on its ingredients. Cognac gives the drink a bold, slightly sweet, and spiced base. Orange liqueur further highlights the fruity notes of the Cognac and dries out the underlined sweetness, while fresh lemon juice brings it all together to complete the perfect sour-style cocktail. Adding sugar to the rim of the glass is optional, but it definitely adds a touch more sweetness to this fairly dry drink. There are conflicting stories as to where this cocktail was invented, London or Paris, and how it got its name, the most popular story is that it got its name from the sidecar of a motorcycle.

CLASSIC SIDECAR	RIFF SHOTGUN	N—A PASSENGER PRINCESS
GLASSWARE coupe	**GLASSWARE** coupe	**GLASSWARE** rocks
Lemon wedge and sugar, for rim 1½ ounces Cognac ¾ ounce orange liqueur ¾ ounce fresh lemon juice Orange twist, for garnish	Lemon wedge and sugar, for rim 1½ ounces Strawberry Cognac (page 38) ½ ounce Aperol ½ ounce passion fruit liqueur ¾ ounce Acidified Orange Juice (page 34) Fresh strawberry, for garnish	2 ounces unfiltered apple juice ¾ ounce fresh lemon juice ¾ ounce Orange Oleo-Saccharum (page 31) 2 dashes orange bitters Apple slice, for garnish
Using a wedge of lemon, rim half of the outside of your coupe glass and roll it in sugar. In a shaker tin, combine the Cognac, orange liqueur, and lemon juice. Add cubed ice and shake vigorously for 12 seconds. Fine-strain into your sugar-rimmed coupe glass and garnish with an orange twist.	Using a wedge of lemon, rim half of the outside of your coupe glass and roll it in sugar. In a shaker tin, combine the strawberry Cognac, Aperol, passion fruit liqueur, and acidified orange juice. Add cubed ice and shake vigorously for 12 seconds. Fine-strain into your sugar-rimmed coupe and garnish with a strawberry.	In a shaker tin, combine the apple juice, lemon juice, orange oleo-saccharum, and orange bitters. Add cubed ice and shake vigorously for 7 seconds. Fine-strain into a rocks glass over fresh ice and garnish with an apple slice.

 PRO TIP Rim your glass with sugar first and then pop it into the freezer while you make your drink. This will not only chill your glassware but also secure the sugar to the glass so it doesn't fall off with every sip.

Left to right: Sidecar, Passenger Princess, Shotgun

Sour Apple Martini

SOUR APPLE MARTINI

1996
Each recipe makes 1 cocktail

The Sour Apple Martini, otherwise known as the Appletini, was created by bartender Adam Karston at Lola's in West Hollywood in 1996. At the time, vodka was making its way into every drink. The bartender was asked to create a cocktail using vodka and a sour apple liqueur in a neon-green bottle. The color alone caught everyone's attention and the Appletini took off from there. The classic recipe is a touch too sweet for me, which is why I like to swap the sour apple liqueur for an apple-flavored vodka.

CLASSIC SOUR APPLE MARTINI	RIFF HOW 'BOUT THEM APPLES	N—A CORE STRENGTH
GLASSWARE chilled martini	**GLASSWARE** chilled coupe	**GLASSWARE** collins
1½ ounces vodka ¾ ounce sour apple liqueur ½ ounce fresh lemon juice ½ ounce fresh lime juice ½ ounce Simple Syrup (page 26) Apple slice, for garnish	1½ ounces green apple vodka ½ ounce fino sherry ½ ounce elderflower liqueur ¾ ounce fresh lemon juice ½ ounce Simple Syrup (page 26) 2 drops Saline Solution (page 40) 2 dashes celery bitters Apple slice, for garnish	2½ ounces fresh green apple juice ½ ounce fresh lime juice ½ ounce Agave Syrup (page 25) 2 ounces nonalcoholic sparkling apple cider Apple slice, for garnish
In a shaker tin, combine the vodka, sour apple liqueur, lemon juice, lime juice, and simple syrup. Add cubed ice and shake vigorously for 12 seconds. Fine-strain into a chilled martini glass and garnish with an apple slice.	In a shaker tin, combine the green apple vodka, fino sherry, elderflower liqueur, lemon juice, simple syrup, saline solution, and celery bitters. Add cubed ice and shake vigorously for 12 seconds. Fine-strain into a chilled coupe and garnish with an apple slice.	In a shaker tin, combine the green apple juice, lime juice, and agave syrup. Add cubed ice and shake vigorously for 7 seconds. Strain into a collins glass over fresh ice and top with nonalcoholic sparkling apple cider. Garnish with an apple slice.

PRO TIP To keep your apples from turning brown after slicing, place them in a cold water bath with a squeeze of fresh lemon juice. This will slow down the oxidation rate, keeping your apples looking fresh.

THE LAST WORD

1915
Each recipe makes 1 cocktail

The Last Word embodies everything I love about a classic cocktail. There are no homemade ingredients, everything is balanced perfectly in equal parts, and it has inspired so many delicious variations. Created right before the start of Prohibition at the Detroit Athletic Club in 1915, The Last Word is enjoyed today just as it was back then. The easiest way to make this drink your own is by simply swapping out the gin with another base spirit. Use mezcal and it's called a Closing Argument. Overproof rum makes it a Wordsmith. Rye whiskey and it's The Final Word.

CLASSIC THE LAST WORD	RIFF ON MUTE	N—A CHATTY KATHY
GLASSWARE chilled coupe	**GLASSWARE** chilled coupe	**GLASSWARE** chilled coupe
¾ ounce gin ¾ ounce green Chartreuse ¾ ounce Maraschino liqueur ¾ ounce fresh lime juice Cherry, for garnish	¾ ounce white rum ¾ ounce Liquore Strega ¾ ounce orange liqueur ¾ ounce pineapple juice ¾ ounce fresh lime juice Orange twist, for garnish	¾ ounce spirit-free gin ¾ ounce Seedlip Garden 108 nonalcoholic spirit ¾ ounce Rosemary Syrup (page 27) ¾ ounce fresh lime juice Rosemary sprig, for garnish
In a shaker tin, combine the gin, green Chartreuse, Maraschino liqueur, and lime juice. Add cubed ice and shake vigorously for 12 seconds. Fine-strain into a chilled coupe glass and garnish with a cherry.	In a shaker tin, combine the white rum, Strega, orange liqueur, pineapple juice, and lime juice. Add cubed ice and shake vigorously for 12 seconds. Fine-strain into a chilled coupe glass and garnish with an orange twist.	In a shaker tin, combine the spirit-free gin, Seedlip Garden, rosemary syrup, and lime juice. Add cubed ice and shake vigorously for 10 seconds. Fine-strain into a chilled coupe glass and garnish with a rosemary sprig.

PRO TIP Green Chartreuse can sometimes be hard to find. An accessible swap would be Genepy or Liquore Strega. They are both herbal liqueurs that provide the same flavor profile.

Left to right: Chatty Kathy,
The Last Word, On Mute

Tom Collins

TOM COLLINS

1882
Each recipe makes 1 cocktail

The "Collins" is a style of the sour cocktail, accompanied by a lengthener or mixer. The Tom Collins is arguably the most well known, which is a gin sour lengthened with soda water. You have the Dutch Collins, which is made with genever, the Colonel Collins made with bourbon, the Pedro Collins made with light rum, and the list goes on. The tall glass the cocktail is served in is lovingly referred to as a "collins" glass, named after the drink. Cocktail historian David Wondrich speculates that the Collins derived from the gin punches that were popular in the nineteenth century. A man by the name of John Collins claims to have invented the drink at the Limmer's Hotel in London. But, as with many classic cocktails, it is hard to say which is true.

CLASSIC TOM COLLINS	RIFF TOM CAT COLLINS	N–A JOAN COLLINS
GLASSWARE collins	**GLASSWARE** collins	**GLASSWARE** collins
2 ounces gin 1 ounce fresh lemon juice ½ ounce Simple Syrup (page 26) 3 ounces soda water Lemon wheel and cherry, for garnish	1½ ounces gin ½ ounce Aperol ½ ounce Milk Liqueur (page 39) 1 ounce Acidified Grapefruit Juice (page 34) 2 dashes Peychaud's bitters 2½ ounces soda water Grapefruit wheel, for garnish	2 ounces spirit-free gin 1 ounce fresh lemon juice ¾ ounce Lemon Oleo-Saccharum (page 31) 1 dash orange bitters 3 ounces soda water Lemon twist, for garnish
In a shaker tin, combine the gin, lemon juice, and simple syrup. Add cubed ice and shake vigorously for 7 seconds. Strain into a collins glass over fresh ice and top with soda water. Gently stir to incorporate and garnish with a lemon wheel and cherry.	In a shaker tin, combine the gin, Aperol, milk liqueur, acidified grapefruit juice, and Peychaud's bitters. Add cubed ice and shake vigorously for 10 seconds. Fine-strain into a collins glass over fresh ice and top with soda water. Gently stir to incorporate and garnish with a grapefruit wheel.	In a shaker tin, combine the spirit-free gin, lemon juice, lemon oleo-saccharum, and orange bitters. Add cubed ice and shake vigorously for 7 seconds. Strain into a collins glass over fresh ice and top with soda water. Gently stir to incorporate and garnish with a lemon twist.

PRO TIP Less ice in your glass doesn't mean more drink; it often means you're getting more mixer, which ultimately throws off the balance of the drink. Ice is used for a purpose: to keep your drink cold from start to finish, to keep your soda from falling flat, and finally, to add dilution.

WHISKEY SMASH

1887
Each recipe makes 1 cocktail

The Whiskey Smash, Mint Julep, and Whiskey Sour are all incredibly similar cocktails. But what differentiates the Whiskey Smash is its use of the entire lemon. A key component of this cocktail is muddling the lemon wedges not only to get the juice but also to extract the oils from the peels and a bit of the bitterness from the pith. The addition of mint lightens the overall cocktail, making it extremely crushable for even the non–whiskey drinker. The Whiskey Smash made its recipe debut in 1887 in Jerry Thomas's book *The Bartender's Guide*.

CLASSIC WHISKEY SMASH	RIFF RUM SMASH	N–A TROPICAL SMASH
GLASSWARE rocks	**GLASSWARE** rocks	**GLASSWARE** rocks
2 ounces bourbon 3 lemon wedges ¾ ounce Simple Syrup (page 26) 4 fresh mint leaves Mint sprig, for garnish	1½ ounces aged rum ½ ounce peach liqueur 2 lemon wedges 3 peach slices ½ ounce Simple Syrup (page 26) Peach slice, for garnish	1 pineapple wedge 1 mango slice 2 lime wedges ½ ounce Demerara Syrup (page 25) 2 ounces coconut water Coconut flakes, for garnish
In a shaker tin, combine the bourbon, lemon wedges, simple syrup, and mint leaves. Gently muddle the lemon wedges and mint, just enough to break them up. Add cubed ice and shake vigorously for 10 seconds. Fine-strain into a rocks glass over fresh ice and garnish with a mint sprig.	In a shaker tin, combine the aged rum, peach liqueur, lemon wedges, peach slices, and simple syrup. Gently muddle the lemon wedges and peach slices, just enough to break them up. Add cubed ice and shake vigorously for 10 seconds. Fine-strain into a rocks glass over fresh ice and garnish with a peach slice.	In a shaker tin, combine the pineapple wedge, mango slice, lime wedges, demerara syrup, and coconut water. Gently muddle the pineapple, mango, and limes, just enough to break them up. Add cubed ice and shake vigorously for 10 seconds. Fine-strain into a rocks glass over fresh ice and garnish with coconut flakes.

 PRO TIP Don't be overly aggressive when muddling. You just want to express oils and flavor, not pulverize the solids. Be especially careful when muddling mint: if overworked it becomes bitter and slimy.

Left to right: Tropical Smash,
Whiskey Smash, Rum Smash

Left to right: Hot Pants, Denim on Denim, White Linen

WHITE LINEN

2008
Each recipe makes 1 cocktail

There's something about the combination of elderflower and cucumber that just makes your taste buds happy. The White Linen is the perfect "patio pounder." The elderflower lends a touch of sweetness to the vegetal quality of the cucumber, and the gin rounds everything out with its bold botanicals. Created at the Ella Dining Room in Sacramento, this is a crowd-pleaser even for the gin skeptic. If you aren't a fan of gin and want a bit more boldness to your drink, give the Hot Pants a try. The tequila and jalapeño pair perfectly with the elderflower and cucumber.

CLASSIC WHITE LINEN	**RIFF** HOT PANTS	**N—A** DENIM ON DENIM
GLASSWARE rocks	**GLASSWARE** collins	**GLASSWARE** collins
2 ounces gin ½ ounce elderflower liqueur ¾ ounce fresh lemon juice ½ ounce Simple Syrup (page 26) 4 cucumber slices 2 ounces soda water Cucumber ribbon, for garnish	2 ounces blanco tequila ½ ounce elderflower liqueur ¾ ounce fresh lime juice ½ ounce Jalapeño Syrup (page 27) 4 cucumber slices 1 jalapeño slice 1 ounce soda water Tajín-sprinkled cucumber slice, for garnish	2 ounces spirit-free gin 2 ounces fresh cucumber juice ¾ ounce fresh lemon juice ½ ounce Jalapeño Syrup (page 27) 2 ounces soda water Cucumber ribbon, for garnish
In a shaker tin, combine the gin, elderflower liqueur, lemon juice, simple syrup, and cucumber slices. Gently muddle the cucumber, just enough to break it up. Add cubed ice and shake vigorously for 10 seconds. Fine-strain into a rocks glass over fresh ice and top with soda water. Gently stir to incorporate and garnish with a cucumber ribbon.	In a shaker tin, combine the tequila, elderflower liqueur, lime juice, jalapeño syrup, cucumber slices, and jalapeño slice. Gently muddle the cucumber and jalapeño, just enough to break them up. Add cubed ice and shake vigorously for 10 seconds. Fine-strain into a collins glass over fresh ice and top with soda water. Gently stir to incorporate and garnish with a Tajín-sprinkled cucumber.	In a shaker tin, combine the spirit-free gin, cucumber juice, lemon juice, and jalapeño syrup. Add cubed ice and shake vigorously for 10 seconds. Fine-strain into a collins glass over fresh ice and top with soda water. Gently stir to incorporate and garnish with a cucumber ribbon.

 PRO TIP Use a vegetable or "Y-peeler" to make your cucumber ribbons. Peel the cucumber lengthwise and with a flick of the wrist, twirl the cucumber into a tight roll with a pair of tweezers.

ZOMBIE

1930s
Each recipe makes 1 cocktail

In all my years of bartending I can confidently say that no one has ever ordered a Zombie from me. Maybe it's the name that turns people off or the fact that it has A LOT of rum in it. Whatever the reason, it's still a quintessential classic tiki cocktail invented by legendary bartender Donn Beach. Often limited to one per person, the Zombie is not only packed with rum but all the tiki essentials, including Don's Mix—a cinnamon-flavored syrup made with grapefruit juice. I wanted to see if I could turn this monster of a cocktail into a more refined sipper, still with all the tiki flavor. However you wish to experience your Zombie, do it with Donn's philosophy in mind: "If you can't get to paradise, I'll bring it to you."

CLASSIC ZOMBIE	**RIFF** BUGABOO	**N–A** SLEEPWALKER
GLASSWARE tiki glass	**GLASSWARE** chilled Nick & Nora	**GLASSWARE** tiki glass
1½ ounces Jamaican rum 1½ ounces gold rum 1 ounce overproof rum ¾ ounce fresh lime juice ½ ounce Don's Mix ½ ounce Falernum (page 30) 1 teaspoon grenadine 4 dashes Pernod 1 dash Angostura bitters Mint sprig, for garnish	2 ounces aged rum ¾ ounce oloroso sherry ¼ ounce pineapple liqueur ¼ ounce Falernum (page 30) ¼ ounce Grapefruit Oleo-Saccharum (page 31) 2 dashes Liquore Strega 2 drops Saline Solution (page 40) 2 dashes Angostura bitters Grapefruit twist and grated cinnamon, for garnish	2 ounces spirit-free rum ½ ounce Falernum (page 30) ½ ounce Grapefruit Oleo-Saccharum (page 31) ¾ ounce fresh lime juice 2 ounces ginger beer Grapefruit wedge, for garnish
In a shaker tin, combine all the rums, the lime juice, Don's Mix, falernum, grenadine, Pernod, and Angostura bitters. Add ½ cup of pebble ice and whip shake (see Pro Tip) for 12 seconds. "Dirty dump" the entire contents of the shaker tin into a tiki glass. Top with more pebble ice and garnish with a mint sprig.	In a mixing glass, combine the aged rum, oloroso sherry, pineapple liqueur, falernum, grapefruit oleo-saccharum, Strega, saline solution, and Angostura bitters. Add cubed ice and stir for no fewer than 30 rotations. Strain into a chilled Nick & Nora glass and garnish with a grapefruit twist and grated cinnamon.	In a shaker tin, combine the spirit-free rum, falernum, grapefruit oleo-saccharum, and lime juice. Add cubed ice and shake vigorously for 10 seconds. Strain into a tiki glass over pebble ice and top with ginger beer. Gently stir to incorporate and garnish with a grapefruit wedge.

PRO TIP There are a few different cocktail shaking styles, a whip shake being one of them. This is when you add a small amount of ice to a cocktail shaker and shake until the entirety of the ice has melted.

Left to right: Bugaboo, Zombie, Sleepwalker

ACKNOWLEDGMENTS

WHERE TO START?

My heartfelt thanks go out to Stephanie Winter, my book agent, who believed in this project wholeheartedly and pushed for it to be published. Kim Keller, Cristina Garces, Emma Campion, and Annie Marino at Ten Speed Press and Andrea Magyar at Penguin Canada took a chance on a first-time author and helped bring my recipes to life. Jayme Lang, my photographer and friend of twenty years, captured the beauty of these cocktails and shared a glimpse into my spirited world. My friends at Cocktail Emporium supplied such beautiful barware and cocktail accouterments. The Keefer Bar and Kodama Ice Co. supplied me with an endless amount of ice. All my friends and family pitched in to taste-test cocktails and help wash glassware, especially my number one barback, my mom. Thanks to my partner, Emily, for her countless words of encouragement that kept me motivated. Lastly, thanks to everyone who has been following and supporting the Like·a·ble cocktail journey. Without you there would be no book.

My grandma was famous for always saying, "We should write a book."

WELL, GRANDMA, WE DID IT!

INDEX

Note: Page references in *italics* indicate photographs.

Tᴇɴ Sᴘᴇᴇᴅ Pʀᴇss
An imprint of the Crown Publishing Group
A division of Penguin Random House LLC
1745 Broadway
New York, NY 10019
tenspeed.com
penguinrandomhouse.com

Copyright © 2025 by Kaitlyn Stewart
Photographs copyright © 2025 by Jayme Lang
Penguin Random House values and supports copyright. Copyright fuels creativity, encourages diverse voices, promotes free speech, and creates a vibrant culture. Thank you for buying an authorized edition of this book and for complying with copyright laws by not reproducing, scanning, or distributing any part of it in any form without permission. You are supporting writers and allowing Penguin Random House to continue to publish books for every reader. Please note that no part of this book may be used or reproduced in any manner for the purpose of training artificial intelligence technologies or systems.

Tᴇɴ Sᴘᴇᴇᴅ Pʀᴇss and the Ten Speed Press colophon are registered trademarks of Penguin Random House LLC.

Typefaces: Milieu Grotesque's Maison Neue, Latinotype's Spirits, Taylor Penton's TAY Makawao, and In-House International's Zanco

Library of Congress Cataloging-in-Publication Data
Names: Stewart, Kaitlyn, author. Title: Three cheers : cocktails three ways: classics, riffs, and zero-proof sips / Kaitlyn Stewart. Identifiers: LCCN 2024044407 (print) | LCCN 2024044408 (ebook) | ISBN 9780593835722 (hardcover) | ISBN 9780593835739 (ebook) Subjects: LCSH: Cocktails. | LCGFT: Cookbooks. Classification: LCC TX951 .S845 2025 (print) | LCC TX951 (ebook) | DDC 641.87/4—dc23/eng/20241029
LC record available at https://lccn.loc.gov/2024044407
LC ebook record available at https://lccn.loc.gov/2024044408

ISBN 978-0-593-83572-2
eBook ISBN 978-0-593-83573-9

Acquiring editors: Kim Keller and Andrea Magyar | Project editors: Kim Keller, Andrea Magyar, and Cristina Garces | Production editor: Patricia Shaw
Designer: Annie Marino | Art director: Emma Campion
Production designers: Mari Gill and Faith Hague
Production: Jessica Heim
Prop stylist: Kaitlyn Stewart | Prop stylist assistant: Jayme Lang
Recipe developer: Kaitlyn Stewart
Copy editor: Kate Slate | Proofreaders: Anne Cherry and Tess Rossi
Indexer: Elizabeth T. Parson
Publicist: Natalie Yera-Campbell | Marketer: Andrea Portanova

Manufactured in China

10 9 8 7 6 5 4 3 2 1

First Edition

The authorized representative in the EU for product safety and compliance is Penguin Random House Ireland, Morrison Chambers, 32 Nassau Street, Dublin D02 YH68, Ireland, https://eu-contact.penguin.ie.

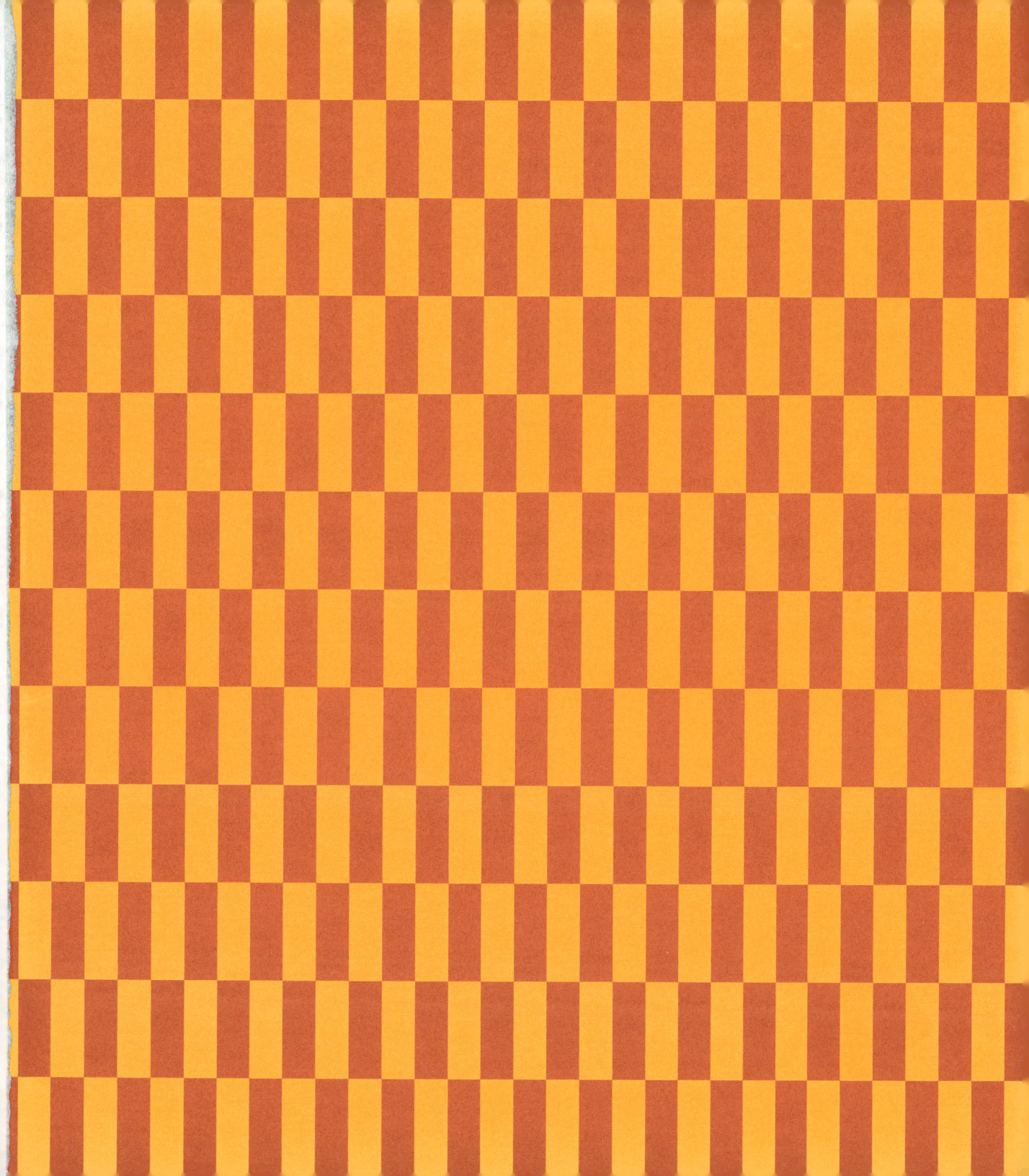

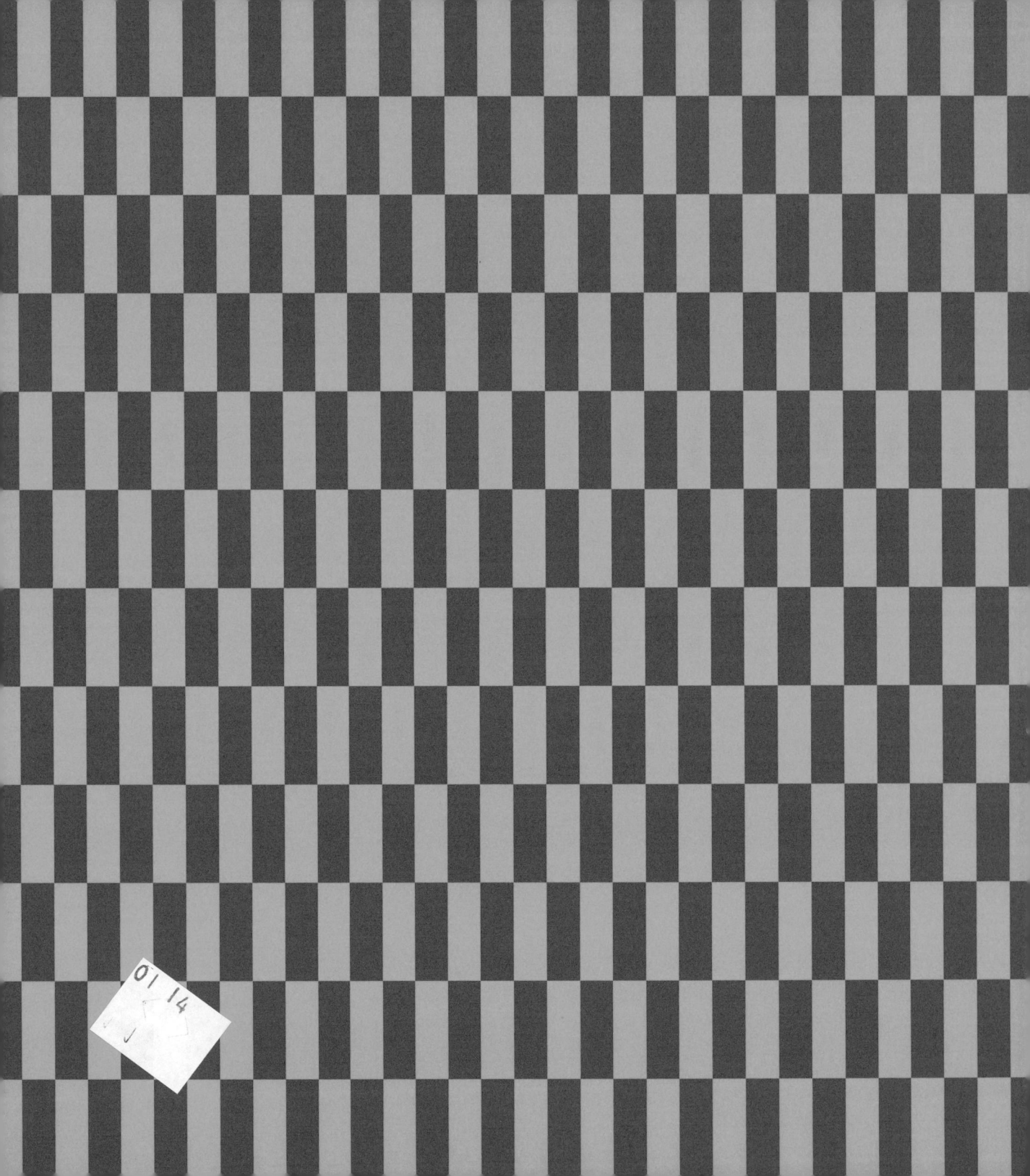